The New York Agent Book

Get the Agent you need for the career you want

9th edition

K CALLAN

Ninth Edition 2012

Other Editions 1987, 1990, 1993, 1995, 1998, 2001, 2003, 2008
ISBN 978-1-878355-22-5
ISSN 1058-1928

Illustrations: Katie Maratta
Editor: Kurt: Quinn
Photographer: Alan Weissman

➤ Read the Directions ➤

Directors, producers, agents and civilians (people not in the business) frequently comment to me that my books about the entertainment industry follow a circuitous route. Actors never say that. They know the business *is* a circuitous route. You enter the circle anyplace and usually don't get to choose where. It is possible to spend twenty years at this occupation and still feel like a beginner, depending on what phase of the career you are experiencing.

The periods of heat in a career make an actor think he will never be unemployed again (no matter what he has witnessed or experienced before) and the periods of unemployment produce only a different agitated state: *I'll never work again. It was all an accident. Now, they know I can't act. I just fooled them before.*

Some young actors waltz in, get attention, an agent and a job, and aren't seriously unemployed for ten or twenty years. When things inevitably slow down, they have to learn the business skills that other less fortunate actors began to learn on day one. There are no steps to be skipped as it turns out. We all just take them at different times.

As important as business skills is self-knowledge. Although some actors never have to find a niche for themselves, most of us spend several years figuring out just what it is we have to sell. If you weigh 500 pounds, it doesn't take a master's degree to figure out that you're going to play the fat one. If you go on a diet and become a more average size, casting directors will have a harder time pegging which one you are and you may, too. This is not to say that if you are easily typed that your life is a bed of roses, but it can be a lot easier.

So, *Self-Knowledge* could be the first chapter for one actor and the end of the book for another. An actor who already has an agent might feel justified in starting with chapter eleven because he wants to change agents while a newcomer in town might feel that divorce is not the problem he's currently confronted with. At this point, all he wants is an agent — any agent.

In fact, a beginning actor would gain insight from chapter eleven. That information could alert him to potential warning signs when he *is* meeting with an agent and chapter two might prompt the seasoned actor to reexamine all the things his agent does do for him.

This book deals with all aspects of actor/agent relationships at various stages of one's career: the first agent, the freelance alliance, the exclusive relationship, confronting the agent with problems, salvaging the bond, and if need be, leaving the partnership.

There is information for the newcomer, help for the seasoned actor and encouragement for everybody. Interviewing hundreds of agents in New York and Los Angeles was just like every other part of the business, sometimes scary, sometimes wonderful and sometimes painful, but always a challenge.

Mostly, the agents were funny, interesting, dynamic, warm and not at all as unapproachable as they seem when you are outside the office looking in.

Regardless of the circuitous nature of the business and this book, my strong advice to you is to read *straight through* and not skip around. The first part provides background to critically understanding the information in the latter part of the book.

Fight the urge to run to the agency listings and read about this agent or that. Until you digest more criteria regarding evaluating agents you may find yourself just as confused as before.

If you read the agents' words with some perception, you will gain insights not only into their character but into how the business really runs. You will notice whose philosophy coincides with yours. Taken by themselves the quotations might only be interesting, but considered in context and played against the insights of other agents, they are revealing and educational.

I have quoted a few agents that you will not find listed here because they are either from Los Angeles, out of the business or deceased. Even though you won't be able to consider them as possible business partners, I felt their insights were particularly valuable, but since they are no longer available as agents, I have listed them in the Index as Mentors.

Check all addresses before mailing. Every effort has been made to provide accurate and current addresses and phone numbers, but agents move and computers goof. Call the office and verify the address, and make sure the agent you want to contact is still there.

It's been a gratifying experience to come in contact with all the agents and all the actors I have met as a result of my books. Because I am asking the questions for all of us, if I've missed something you deem important, tell me and I'll include it in my next book. Write to me c/o Sweden Press at the address on the back of the book, or at my e-mail address: Kcallan@swedenpress.com. Be sure to write something in the reference line that identifies you as a reader; I dump a lot of junk mail.

K Callan
Los Angeles, California

✒ Table of Contents ✒

1. Forewarned. 1
    Changes in the business since the last edition. SAG-AFTRA .
    Changes in the business in general.

2. Before you Leave Home. 3
    Things you can do in your own home town. Where to study. The
    cool schools.

3   Welcome to the Big Apple. 11
    How to organize yourself for life as an actor in New York: from
    conservatory programs to classes in New York, from apartment
    hunting to support groups, to survival jobs and more.

4   Your First Agent and His Tools. 15
    Preparing to agent yourself. Choosing the right photographer.
    Pictures. Building and formatting a resume. The actor's primary
    job: looking for work.

5. Self-Knowledge. 45
    How the business really works. Who gets hired and why.
    Analyzing your strengths and weaknesses. Learning about
    process.

6. Avenues of Opportunity. 58
    Researching agents. Tools to get and set up meetings. How to
    behave when you get there and after. What to ask. What to look
    for. Knowing an agent's responsibilities and background
    prepares you to choose and attract the agent that is right for
    you.

7. Kinds of Representation. 64
    The pros and cons of exclusive vs freelance representation. The
    differences between a theatrical and commercial resume. Dealing
    with Paragraph 6.

8.   Research and Follow-through............... 68

Researching agents. Tools to get and set up meetings. How to behave when you get there and after. What to ask for, what to look for.

9.   Star/Conglomerate Agencies.............. 82

Corporate agencies have more money, clout and access. What is the downside? Does it matter to casting directors where they find you? What are the perks of representation by independent agencies?

10.   What Everybody Wants.................... 90

Agents and actors are looking for the same thing: a partner who will make them rich and famous. Having realistic expectations of your agent and holding up your part of the bargain will carry you far. Understanding the true meaning of the 90%-10% equation.

11.   Everybody's Responsibilities................ 97

Being successful in business depends on the energy expended by all parties as well as their focus and determination. Having realistic expectations of your agent and holding up your part of the bargain will carry you far. Understanding the true meaning of the 90%/10% equation.

12.   Stand-Ups/Children. 110

How stand-up performers access the business and what they need to do so. Understanding why your child shouldn't be in the business, but if you're going to do it anyway, understanding the parent's role in the equation and the best way to go about it.

13.   Managers.. 116

Managers are agents without restrictions who charge more. Why do you need one? What are their legal restrictions? Who benefits from having a manager.? Why the Breakdown Service is a tool for agents only. Understanding Top of Show/Major Role work designations. The importance of a good showbiz reference library and a beginning reading list.

14. Divorce.................................... 123

Reasons to leave and reasons to stay. If you must leave, how to do it as an adult and with some class.

15. Researching the Agents.................... 132

How to read the agency profiles. What to look for. The importance of referrals.

16. Agency Listings........................... 138

17. Glossary................................... 203

18. Indexes.................................... 209

Index to Agents & Agencies........................ 210
Index to Agents for Children...................... 217
Index to Agents for Stand-up...................... 217
Index to Agents for Young Adults.................. 218
Index to Everything Else.......................... 219
Index to Mentors.................................. 221
Index to Photographers............................ 221
Index to Resources................................ 221
Index to Teachers................................. 221
Endnotes.. 222

⚒ 1 ⚒

Forewarned

As this 9th edition goes to press, the two biggest pieces of news are that the Screen Actors Guild and The American Federation of Television and Radio Artists have finally merged creating SAG-AFTRA and that New York continues to build as a film and television production center. In 2010-2011, New York state was home to 372 key projects including 234 films and 138 television series.

In that same time period, The Broadway theatre season scored its highest grossing season on record.

The bad news is that the new media is still formatting itself financially, so even though it's easier than ever to get your face out to the world, figuring out how to make money off your venture is still a work in progress, even for the studios and networks.

Old news is that reality shows continue to dominate the airways. According the to the Nielsen ratings of June 25, 2012, reality shows took the five top rating slots as well as #9 and #10. It's true that the Olympic trials took three of those nights, but *America's Got Talent* took the other two slots. On cable, seven out of ten were reality shows of one kind or another. That includes two slots filled by sports.

www.nielsen.com/us/en/insights/top10s/television.html

Ultimately the financial pie will be more in our favor online and while the thirst for reality shows may never diminish for a certain segment of the population, history shows that the pendulum swings both directions and scripted shows will always be relevant.

As with any business, the way to survive and prosper is to see how you can manipulate the energy of the marketplace to your advantage. If you were a saddle maker when automobiles were invented, you could whine and ask for a subsidy or you could figure out how to adapt your business to the new world.

That's what actors have to do now. Perhaps you'll be lucky and find a place in the marketplace without adapting, but maybe there is a way for you to create a show that will fit into the current climate.

Oprah Winfrey studied to be an actress, switched to media and began a career as a broadcaster which, among countless other showbiz accomplishments, led to an Academy Award nomination for *The Color Purple*. *How I Met Your Mother* stars Jason Segel and Josh Radnor spend their hiatus' not only starring in films, but Radnor wrote, directed and starred in *Happythankyoumoreplease* as well as his latest, *Liberal Arts*. Segal wrote and starred in the hits *The Muppets, The Five-Year Engagement* and *Forgetting Sarah Marshall* and Neil Patrick Harris, of course does *every*thing. And these are people who already *have* regular jobs.

You never know where your entrepreneurial talents will take you. The one thing we know is true, however, is that an investment of positive energy always pays off.

With that in mind, whether you're just starting in the business and trying to figure out your first step, or whether you find yourself suddenly agent-free, take heart and take a big breath. Anything is possible.

Let's begin.

Good News

✓ SAG-AFTRA
✓ more opportunities in New York
✓ the net continues of offer opportunities and experience

Bad News

✓ new media not financially viable yet

⚔ 2 ⚔

Before You Leave Home

Three tools you need to bring with you to Manhattan are experience, education and money.

I would think most anyone who plans to assault the major marketplaces as an actor would have started acting in school plays and taken pretty much every chance to get up in front of people in their own home town.

That includes any acting related ventures, whether it's singing The Star Spangled Banner at local baseball games, doing local television and radio commercials, producing podcasts, webisodes or short films or just generally being the center of any entertainment related ventures.

If you are still home and haven't been doing that, it's not too late. There is much to be learned in your local marketplace. If you're not far enough along to create your own projects, scour the newspaper and internet looking for productions filming locally looking for help. Even working as a gofer will yield a wealth of information and experince.

You might think these kinds of credits wouldn't count for much in Manhattan, but not only will they grow you as an actor and entrepreneur, that information on your resume shows your determination to learn all parts of the business and makes you a more attractive potential business partner to an agent.

If you're reading this book about getting an agent before you've trained, you pretty much have the cart before the horse, but if you are still thinking about where to train, here is a mouth-watering list.

The Cool Schools

This list of the Top 25 Drama Schools is from *The Hollywood Reporter* and is based on info from top casting directors. I'm just listing edited highlights here. Do check out the full list online for the full scoop: *www.hollywoodreporter.com/news/top-25-drama-schools-319963*

American Conservatory Theatre in San Francisco MFA boasts a resident company of top-notch professional actors. It is part of those actors' job to mentor and network for the MFA students. In turn, MFA students mentor kids in the Young Conservatory program (YC alumni include Darren Criss, Winona Ryder and Nicolas Cage). Students also audition for real-world ACT productions -- and get cast. Notable Alumni: Elizabeth Banks, Annette Bening, Delroy Lindo, Anna Deavere Smith, Denzel Washington.

The Actors Studio, Pace University in New York is not just a place for celebs to promote their latest accomplishments. Curriculum and faculty are chosen by Actors Studio Drama School presidents Al Pacino, Harvey Keitel and Ellen Burstyn. Even so, the listed Notable Alumni list is small: Bradley Cooper, Chris Stack and Xanthe Elbrick.

California Institute of the Arts (Calarts) in Valencia, California may not be as well known as some of these other names, but notable alumni include Don Cheadle, Ed Harris, Condola Rashad, Eliza Coupe, Alison Brie and Katey Sagal.

Carnegie Mellon in Pittsburgh has long been praised for its extensive training and notable Alumni: Ted Danson, Rob Marshall, Steven Bochco, Paula Wagner, Patrick Wilson, John Wells.

Depaul University in Chicago benefits from being in what some consider the nation's second-best theater town. The 6-to-1 student-faculty ratio helps, too. Notable Alumni: Gillian Anderson, Kevin Anderson, Judy Greer, Karl Malden, Joe Mantegna, Elizabeth Perkins, John C. Reilly.

Florida State University in Sarasota, Florida boasts these amazing perks. All 12 of the Florida State University/Asolo Conservatory MFA candidates get a full tuition waiver from Florida State University, an assistantship to defray living expenses, a year's study in London, experience at the Asolo Theater and Actors' Equity union eligibility. Notable Alumni: Paul Reubens.

Guildhall School of Music & Drama in London is so sought after that *Downton Abbey*'s Michelle Dockery says, "Getting in was like winning the lottery." Notable Alumni: Daniel Craig, Ewan McGregor, Joseph Fiennes, Rhys Ifans, Eileen Atkins, Orlando Bloom.

The Juilliard School in New York may be painful, challenging and confusing, but as alumna Laura Linney says, "This school will prepare you for just about anything." A major theater director says, "In language skill and script analysis, no other grads are as prepared. Juilliard actors somehow are more marketable -- the first-round draft picks." Notable Alumni: Viola Davis, Kevin Spacey, Robin Williams, Jessica Chastain, Kevin Kline, Patti LuPone, Kelsey Grammar.

London Academy of Music and Dramatic Arts (LAMDA) in London has been producing Oscar, Golden Globes, Olivier Awards, BAFTAs and Tony winners since 1861. Notable Alumni: John Lithgow, Donald Sutherland, Jim Broadbent, Brian Cox, Swoosie Kurtz.

National Institute of Dramatic Art in Kensington (NIDA) Australia admits only 4 percent of its applicants. "I mean, I loved NIDA and hated it," Mel Gibson says in a documentary about the school. "At times, it was very frustrating and hard and depressing and all this kind of stuff, but if you were prepared to stick with it, the rewards were really good." Notable Alumni: Cate Blanchett, Judy Davis, Baz Luhrmann, Hugo Weaving.

Northwestern University in Evanston, Illinois undergraduate drama program puts acting in a liberal-arts context. Notable Alumni: Warren Beatty, Zach Braff, Seth Meyers, Ann-Margret, David Schwimmer.

Tisch School of the Arts at Nyu in New York City benefits from its proximity to the big time. "When Mike Nichols revives Death of a Salesman, NYU probably knows very early and knows who's casting," says one producer. Notable Alumni: Alec Baldwin, Philip Seymour Hoffman, Michael C. Hall, Jeremy Piven.

Royal Academy of Dramatic Art (RADA) in London deserves its royal reputation. Some classes involve one teacher and three students. The Beatles are famous because their RADA-trained manager, Brian Epstein, taught them to be dramatic. RADA can put talented nobodies on the radar. Notable Alumni: Anthony Hopkins, Peter O'Toole, Joan Collins, Maggie Gyllenhaal, Ralph Fiennes, Vivien Leigh, Mike Leigh.

Rutgers University in New Brunswick, New Jersey. The acting BFA program at Rutgers University accepts 9 percent of applicants, who spend their third year at Shakespeare's Globe Theatre in London. Both BFAs and MFAs do annual showcase performances in New York. Notable Alumni: Calista Flockhart, Sebastian Stan, James Tupper, Kristin Davis.

State University of New York, Purchase in Purchase, New York. The Conservatory of Theatre Arts BFA acting program at SUNY's Purchase College is run by Gregory Taylor, an eminent film scholar. Notable Alumni: Edie Falco, Parker Posey, Stanley Tucci.

Syracuse University in Syracuse, N.Y. In 1978, says Syracuse drama professor Geraldine Clark, the BFA program attracted 250 applicants. "Now we get 900 a year. Our grads are noted for being sui generis." Aaron Sorkin started as Clark's musical-theater student. The key to the program: student access to the Syracuse Stage, a theater enticing 90,000 playgoers a year. Notable Alumni: Frank Langella, Taye Diggs.

University of Delaware in Newark, Delaware. Students of Delaware's Professional Theatre Training Program get tuition waivers and a $16,500 stipend. "It has only one class of students at a time, and each gets full attention," says its director, Sanford Robbins. Notable Alumni: Tom Hewitt, Linda Balgord.

University of California at Los Angeles (UCLA) in Los Angeles, California. UCLA BA and BFA drama students benefit by being at a red-hot center of the study of film, TV, animation and digital media and close to Hollywood. Notable Alumni: Tim Robbins, Eric Roth, Nicolas Cage, Jack Black.

University of North Carolina School of the Arts in Winston-Salem, North Carolina is helmed by ex-New York Shakespeare Festival artistic director Gerald Freedman. He has created an undergrad drama program where students get guest instruction from the likes of Sam Waterston, Patrick Wilson and UNC alums Mary-Louise Parker and Chris Parnell. Notable Alumni: Joe Mantello, Tom Hulce.

University of California at San Diego (UCSD) in San Diego is home to the Tony-winning La Jolla Playhouse, San Diego. Notable Alumni: Danny Burstein, James Avery.

University of Southern California School of Dramatic Arts (USC) in Los Angeles. USC acting students are trained in TV, feature films and, internet work. Notable Alumni: Forest Whitaker, Swoosie Kurtz, Eric Stoltz, Kyra Sedgwick.

University of Texas at Austin in Austin, Texas. UT acting students get a boost from Austin's famous film festival and independent film scene. Robert Rodriquez shoots and casts most of his films from there. Notable Alumni: Marcia Gay Harden.

University of Washington in Seattle, Washington. Half of Washington's Professional Actors program students find work within a year of graduation (e.g., Kyle MacLachlan and his first movie, *Dune*), and half are still performing 10 years after graduation. Notable Alumni: Jean Smart, Joel McHale, Pamela Reed, Rainn Wilson.

Western Australian Academy of Performing Arts in Perth, Western Australia. Actors put on 300 performances a year at WAAPA, and the experience pays off. "I am totally indebted to WAAPA for [my] career," says alum Hugh Jackman. "There is a genuine camaraderie. Acting is not a solo sport." Notable Alumni: Frances O'Connor.

Yale University School of Drama in New Haven, Connecticut is generally considered the most prestigious U.S. drama school. Notable Alumni: Meryl Streep, Paul Giamatti, Paul Newman, Patricia Clarkson, Frances McDormand.

Staff, *Hollywood Reporter*[1]

In the past, the *HR* seemed to only cover movie grosses and the information seemed to be mainly for producers and star actors, but recently, it has turned into a rich source of information for actors at all stages of their careers. I recommend reading it regularly.

The Hollywood Reporter list not withstanding, many agents concur that the two best musical theatre programs in the country belong to the Cincinnati Conservatory of Music and the Boston Conservatory of Music. Each year, these schools' industry showcases attract almost every agent and casting director in New York City. Their graduates probably have the highest employment percentage of ANY drama school, musical or otherwise, graduate or undergraduate.

✦ *Although the connected schools may sometimes lead to auditions for immediate employment on a soap opera, in summer stock, in an off-Broadway play, more often it serves as a casting director's mental Rolodex of actors to use in future projects.*
Jill Gerston, *New York Times*[2]

✦ *Your first year out of one of those school, we can get you a lot of opportunities, it's up to you to prove yourself.*
Don Birge/*Stewart Talent*

Even if you are educated at the best schools and arrive highly touted with interest from agents, ex-William Morris agent Joanna Ross told me there is still a period of adjustment.

✦ *When you come out of school, you gotta freak out for a while. Actors in high-powered training programs working night and day doing seven different things at once get out of school and suddenly there is no demand for their energy. It takes a year, at least, to learn to be unemployed. And they have to learn to deal with that. It happens to everybody. It's not just you.*
Joanna Ross/former William Morris agent

Even if you can't make it to a league school, all is not lost.

✦ *The truth is, a great performance in a connected school can jump-start a career, but if these kids have talent, they'll get noticed. They just won't be as fast out of the starting gate...they just have to do it the old-fashioned way by pounding the pavements, reading "Back Stage," calling up friends, going to see directors they know and knocking on agents' doors.*

Jill Gerston, New York Times[3]

And maybe faster out of the gate isn't the best way to go anyway. Success in any business takes a toll on the persona. The more maturity you can gain first, the better your chance of weathering the shock of lots of money, instant friends and visibility. It's easier to deal with success when it comes gradually so you can adapt.

Too much too soon is too much too soon. No matter who you are, the career ebbs and flows. Stardom is just unemployment at a higher rate of pay.

And speaking of pay brings up the third important tool to bring with you to New York: money. You need an emergency fund and a conservative approach to your money or you could set your career back a few years just digging out.

A cautionary and educational tale about a young actor and his money can be found in the archives of my monthly column at *www.actorsink.com*. It's too long to print here, but if you can actually hear the message at this stage of your life, it could make a big difference to you across the board. Or you might just have to learn the hard way, but just in case, it's worth the effort to check out "The Actor and Money." *https://www.nowcasting.com/actorsink/article.php?articleID=3428&lastupdate=1341622279*

Start listening to money guru Dave Ramsey (*www.daveramsey.com*) on the radio or check out his webpage. His philosophy would serve you well.

Wrap Up

Experience

- ✓ school plays
- ✓ local showbiz experience
- ✓ local civic events
- ✓ local radio and television commercials
- ✓ your own creations

Training

- ✓ connected schools helpful but can only do so much
- ✓ if you are trained and determined, everything evens out, it may just take longer

Money

- ✓ have emergency fund
- ✓ learn how to manage money
- ✓ Dave Ramsey

⇗ 3 ⇖

Welcome to the Big Apple

Now that you've exhausted all the opportunities at home, gotten yourself trained and created an emergency fund, you are finally ready to tackle Manhattan. As training for the impossible challenge of making a living as an actor, your first task will be to get acquainted with the city and get a place to live in New York.

Getting to Know the City

It's easy to get around the island of Manhattan. If you are directionally challenged, this is your chance to finally understand about north, south, east, and west. The Hudson River is west and guess where the East River is?

As you travel uptown (north), the numbers get larger and as you go downtown toward Wall Street, Chinatown, and the Statue of Liberty (south), the numbers get smaller. The numbers stop at Houston Street (pronounced "how-ston") and become Delancey, Spring, etc.

The next quickest way to get anywhere is on a bicycle, if you have the courage. That's too scary for me, so I walk. Cabs are expensive and frequently very slow. The fastest transportation is the subway which requires MetroCards. You can buy them at banks, some newsstands and in machines at most subway stations. Many stations don't have manned token booths at all times, so have appropriate bills or a credit card and don't expect directions.

There are subways that only go up and down the East Side (Lexington Avenue) and some that only go up and down the West Side (7th Avenue) and some (the E & F) that do both. There are some that only go crosstown (14th Street, 42nd Street and 59th Street). For more info: *www.mta.info/nyct/subway/*.

Both the iPhone and Androids have awesome apps that tell you where the closest subway is and how to get where you are going. Download one first thing, but don't get dependent on them, you need to learn your way around.

Buses are great for shorter hops and accept Metrocards or exact change. For more information about NY buses: *www.mta.info/nyct/bus/howto_bus.htm/a/metrocards.htm*

I can walk across town in about twenty minutes; you probably can too. Crosstown blocks go east and west and are about three times as long as downtown blocks which go north and south. It takes about the same amount of time to walk from 42nd to 59th Streets as it takes to go from Lexington Avenue to Broadway.

In order to find the nearest cross street for your destination, check *www.google.com/maps* or *www.ny.com/locator*. For general New York City transportation info try *www.travel.howstuffworks.com/new-york-city-guide1*.

Another way to get a handful of excellent Manhattan information is to pick up *The Official City Guide*, available at most hotels and/or online at *www.cityguideny.com*. I don't think I've seen a better source of maps and information about what's going on in Manhattan. It includes useful phone numbers and a reference page detailing cross streets relative to the address. Another useful link is *www.newyorkcity.com*.

Get a Place to Live

Even though it's New York, the problem is not unsolvable. The Drama Book Shop (250 West 40th Street), most acting schools and the acting unions all have bulletin boards listing sublets that might give you temporary housing while you get your bearings. Another good housing resource is *www.craigslist.com*.

There is actor-friendly housing in West Beth (downtown in the West Village) and The Manhattan Plaza (midtown on the West Side). Both are artistic communities with subsidized housing and long waiting lists, but since actors are frequently out of town for jobs, sublets are available. Both of these artists' havens offer classes and are plugged into the creative forces of the city.

Areas in which rents might be cheaper are the Lower East Side, below Wall Street, Chinatown, Harlem, the Upper West Side and some areas of what used to be called Hell's Kitchen in the far West 40s.

The city has a center to help people find affordable housing, *www.nyc.gov/html/housinginfo/html/home/home.shtml*. There is also a youth hostel. For information consult the Visitors Bureau at *www.nycgo.com*.

There are those fabled $400 per month apartments that keep us all salivating but they have been occupied for hundreds of years by the same tenant. Don't stop yourself from finding suitable housing because you are waiting for one of those mythical deals. You don't want to use up all your good luck getting a swell apartment for 35¢. Save your luck for your big break and you'll be able to afford to pay full price.

More people are finding housing in Brooklyn, Queens, New Jersey and Staten Island. When I arrived in New York, I briefly considered New Jersey (since I had children), but after much soul-searching, I realized that my dream was to come to New York City. I decided that if I was going to starve, it would be while living my dream all the way. Not everyone's dream is so particularized. These days, it's very cool to live in Brooklyn.

The next thing you need to do is to get a job, and not just for financial survival.

A Job Gives Form to Your Life

Having a job gives form to your life, a place to go every day, a family of people to relate to and helps you feel as though you are part of the city and not just a tourist.

Nothing feeds depression more than sitting at home alone in a strange city. Even if you know your way around, you'll find that as time goes on, activity is the friend of the actor. Depression feeds on itself and must not be allowed to get out of hand.

Don't drain your emergency fund. If you allow yourself to be broke you'll just drag yourself down. This is something you can control. Being a starving actor doesn't work. What works is to take care of yourself so that you are healthy and have money in your pocket and not eternally worried about paying your bills. Don't keep taking money from your parents, be responsible for yourself and get a job.

✦ *Before an actor begins to look for an agent, he should establish a secure foundation. He or she needs a place to live and/or a job, some friends to talk to, and pictures or at least a facsimile of pictures. It's very important that they have a comfortable place to go to during the day and be settled so they don't carry any more anxiety than necessary into an agent or manager's office.*

Some actors think an agent or a manager will turn into a surrogate mother-father-teacher-confessor. That isn't his role. Actors get disappointed when they aren't taken care of right away. I think it's better to come in as a fully secure person so you can be sold that way. Otherwise, too much development time is wasted.

Gary Krasny/The Krasny Office

✦ *If you can combine a showbiz job with flexible hours permitting auditions, that's the best of all possibilities. Always be available. Don't say you are an actor if you have a 9-to-5 job. If you must waitress, do it at night.*

Sharon Carry/Carry Company

Casting Society of America Job File

Sitting in an agent's office waiting for an appointment, I met a young actor who was manning the phones. He told me he has worked as a casting assistant in both Los Angeles and New York and had come to his present job by faxing his resume to the Casting Society of America job file.

The pay is small, but as he pointed out, the access to the business was well worth it. He said he wouldn't trade a higher salary for the business maturity he had acquired.

I visited the CSA's website recently and found links pertaining to Diversity Showcases, an ABC Talent Showcase, and many other items of interest to actors. Although you can also search for a particular casting director's name, if you don't know any names, you can't search; there is no master list. I also found a link called "Invite a CD," with an option to send a virtual postcard to casting directors inviting them to showcases, screenings, comedy appearances, etc.

Casting Society of America
2565 Broadway, #185
New York, NY 10025
212-868-1260 Ext. 22
www.castingsociety.com

As soon as you are working in the business in any category, you are in the system and on your way. I don't want to imply that coming up with one of these jobs is the easiest task in the world, but it is definitely worth the effort.

Before your resume is ready for you to be interviewing agents as possible business partners, you may find yourself encountering them either in your work or on a social level. Just as doctors don't like to listen to your symptoms at a party, an agent wants to party in peace. Be a professional and talk about something other than your career. Agents prefer to do business in their offices. If you detect signs of interest from anyone, directors, producers, etc., follow up on it. Ask if there is anything you can do to help with a current project.

I know you are itching to look for an agent and become a working actor, but first things first; get situated, meet some people, fill up your energy/good feelings and financial bank accounts. You will need them all.

Wrap Up

Geographical Resources

✓ maps
✓ NYC Convention Bureau
✓ Internet
✓ Google Maps
✓ smart phone apps

Finding a Place to Live

✓ Drama Book Shop bulletin boards
✓ union bulletin boards
✓ *www.craigslist.com*

Your Day Job

✓ gives form to your life
✓ a family
✓ a place to go every day
✓ any showbiz job teaches you about the business

⚐ 4 ⚐

Your First Agent & His Tools

There's good news and bad news. First the bad news: you're probably going to have to be your own first agent. Now the good news: nobody cares more about your career than you do, so your first agent is going to be incredibly motivated.

In order to attract an agent, you have to have something to sell. No matter how talented you are, if you don't have some way to show what you've got, you're all talk. Working up a scene for the agent's office will work for a few agents, but it's not enough.

Your focus should be to amass credits by appearing onstage and in student and independent films so an agent can find you – and so you can put together a professional audition DVD.

This book is focused on actors who are already entrepreneurial. For those who need help in that department, get my marketing book, *How to Sell Yourself as an Actor*.

I know what you are thinking: "Swell. How am I going to amass credits and put together a professional sample without an agent? How am I ever going to get any work? How will I get smarter?"

By growing. Pick up *Back Stage* or *Show Business* for casting notices or go online to their websites. Become part of the actor's grapevine by joining a theatre group or getting into an acting class. Invite a group of actors to your place once a week to read a play aloud. Once you start expending energy in a smart way, things begin to happen. Sending out pictures and resumes is not a growth experience.

✦ *Grab a "Back Stage" and start auditioning for everything! Then find a well-known and respected acting teacher who works with accomplished students. These two small actions will be the beginning of your show business networking. Teachers, friends and colleagues provide a conduit to your future agent or to a casting director.*
Jeanne Nicolosi/Nicolosi & Co., Inc.

I asked dance agent Thomas Scott the first thing dancers should do. His advice works for actors too:

✦ *Start to study and become familiar with the choreographers. Begin to form relationships with working choreographers. Both Broadway Dance Center and Steps are dance studios where great working choreographers teach.*
Thomas Scott/DDO Artists Agency

✦ *Decide what you want to do. Narrow your focus. Do you want to sing? Dance? Be in movies? Be specific, get good headshots, and we'll plan it out and do it together.*
Lisa Price/The Price Group Talent

✦ *They are meeting us for the first time, we shouldn't meet them unless they do something better than a whole lot of other people. This is a town of specialities. Versatility is for grad school, but when you compete as an actor in New York, it's about being special not how many things you do.*
Jed Abrahams/The Talent House

✦ *Gain technique and skill. Nurture your look. You are your own product. Fine tuning your look is the most important thing.*
Thomas Scott/DDO Artists Agency

✦ *Contact everyone you know. Get to class. Get good headshots. If you are "soap" material, send your picture/resume to all the daytime casting directors.*
Diana Doussant/Leading Artists, Inc.

✦ *It's always been hard for someone right out of school. They don't know how tall the mountain is and how far they have to go, it's probably just the same as it usually is when anybody gets to town, they have to adjust to the city, they have to learn to support themselves, they have to learn to adjust to the audition.*
Renee Glicker/About Artists Agency

✦ *There are many different ways for actors to introduce themselves to the industry even when unrepresented. Whether it's a show you have mounted or something you put up on youtube, the important thing to remember is that anything you put out there should be looked upon as an audition for the most important person in the industry.*
Jed Abrahams/The Talent House

You're not going to just waltz in and meet agents and casting executives, but as you begin to make friends with others on your level in the business, you will be surprised how one thing leads to another.

The Actor's Job: Looking for Work

Becoming an actor is not an overnight process. A large part of being an actor on any level is looking for work. Don't equate being paid with being an actor.

You are already an actor. Even if you are a student actor, you're still an actor and you already have your first job: get a resume with decent credits onstage, on film and television. This will begin to season you as an actor, and if it's on camera, you will be building an audition DVD.

What denotes decent credits?

✦ *Expectations for a young actor are different than for an older actor. The white space is your friend, it means you are fresh. Don't fib a lot of experience and try to act older, you need training but your youth and meager resume is what you have to sell.*

Jed Abrahams/The Talent House

That said, your blank resume is probably not going to get you into any offices for them to see how young and fresh you are and though there have been a few young and particularly gorgeous or extremely wacky character people who got called in from blanketing the town with their pictures and blank resumes, that's a rarity.

In lieu of gorgeousness, wackiness or a diploma from one of the connected schools, take a breath and embrace your fate. You must build your resume and your relationships within the business (that means people you work with not those you meet at parties).

If you are able to score a good part in a decent venue that gets reviewed, an agent might see you and/or read your great reviews and agree to take a meeting with you.

If you hope to be cast in film and television you need to be able to deliver an example of your work on DVD. It should be no longer than five minutes (shorter is best) and shows either one performance or a selection of scenes of an actor's work. It's very difficult for an agent to get a casting director to meet you unless there is a sample of your work, so focus on getting film in your bag. Do every independent or student film you can, you need film.

Agents and casting executives view work endlessly and can tell quickly if you are of interest to them, so even if you have some great stuff, err on the side of brevity. It is better to have just one good scene from an actual job than many short moments of work or a scene produced just for the reel. Some agents will watch self-produced work and some will not. Most casting directors tell me that if they have time, they usually watch whatever is sent.

Technology and editors have gotten so skillful that it's easy to come up with a slick package if you have the money, but caution: slickness is no substitute for quality work. Casting directors can tell when it's all just tap dancing.

If you can't produce footage that shows you clearly in contemporary material playing a part that you could logically be cast for, then you aren't far enough along to make a DVD. Better to wait than to show yourself at less than your best. Patience.

What Agents Want in a Picture

The number one dictate about pictures is: What You See Is What You Get. Agents don't like surprises. If your picture looks like Jennifer Lopez and you look like Joan Cusack, the agent not going to be happy when he calls you in to read and you will be disappointed.

Your picture and your DVD are your main selling tools, so choose carefully. Pictures can be printed with or without a border. Some agents prefer a picture without, but borderless frequently costs more. Your name should be printed on the front, either superimposed over the photo or in the white space below. Name and contact information should be featured prominently on the resume and on the bottom right edge of your picture.

Although the majority of actors hand out a closeup, more and more are using a 3/4 color shot. That's the industry standard for dancers.

The picture of you on your mother's piano is not necessarily the best for your selling tool. Be conscious of the jobs you are sent for when you choose your 8x10.

There are many good photographers in town whose business is taking actor headshots. They vary in price and product. I've gathered a list of favorites from agents, actors, and casting directors. Don't just choose one off the list. You need to do your own research on something as personal as a photograph.

The Internet has made shopping for a photographer easier. You can look at a number of pictures and evaluate why one picture appeals to you more than another. An expensive price tag doesn't guarantee a better picture. It's possible to get the perfect picture for under $200 and a picture you will never use at $900.

The consensus from agents seems to be that you should expect to pay $500-$600 for pictures. Photographers encourage hair and makeup, but that's more for them than you. It makes their job easier. Decide for yourself what you want. It's nice to be professionally put together, but make sure you can duplicate the look when you audition.

It takes time to meet personally with several photographers but it's worth the effort. It's not just that you need to meet the photographer, he needs to meet you and get a sense of who you are. My friend Mary's pictures were taken by a respected Los Angeles photographer and though technically perfect, they had a moodiness to them that had nothing to do with Mary's natural affability. The pictures were interesting but did not represent who Mary is and how she is cast.

If you choose the right photographer, you can get appropriate pictures and it can be fun,

✦ *When you schedule your headshot session, you are choosing to make a positive change in your career. It's something you should enjoy doing, and look forward to. Prepare for your shoot by treating yourself well, getting plenty of sleep, caring for your body, and allowing plenty of time to prepare. If you're nervous, bring a friend, and bring music that you like.*

Nick Coleman/photographer

Some actors I know have pictures taken by family members with digital cameras. With Photoshop at your fingertips, you can take out unwanted shadows and produce a pretty good picture on your own, however if you have the money to hire the right professional, it's worth it. Pictures are your agent's selling tools. Give them something that represents you.

And from personal experience, I would like to say, don't get carried away with wanting to look beautiful/handsome unless you are Brad or Angelina. I had some great pictures taken and was totally in love with them. However, when I was able to step back and evaluate, I realized that those pictures, though flattering, were worthless to me. I am pretty, but I'm never going to be cast as "the pretty one", so there is no use in my trying to sell myself that way. One must be realistic.

I take absolute responsibility for that gaff. That photographer didn't really know my work. I had chosen him because his lighting, hair and makeup result in glamorous photos and I was having a vanity attack.

And how do you evaluate the effectiveness of your picture?

✦ *If you are getting a lot of auditions, but aren't booking work, the problem is not your headshot. If you are having trouble getting an agent to open your mail, or getting called into audition for casting directors, the problem could very well be your headshot. Is it high quality? Does it represent you well? Is it recent enough?*

Nick Coleman/photographer

Photographers

Richard Blinkoff shoots, edits, proofs, retouches and prints his digital photos in his daylight studio in Chelsea. He also does any typesetting and graphic work you need to make other headshots, postcards or composite cards. Check out *www.richardblinkoff.com* for his portfolio at 212-620-7883.

Tess Steinkolk sounds great. She graduated from the American University in Washington D.C., a city in which she had an illustrious career not only at the White House during the Carter Administration, but also at the Smithsonian where she studied and was on staff. During that time she was house photographer for the Arena Stage. She moved to New York in 1981 and continues her amazing work.

The FAQ link on Tess' webpage answers every question from how much, to how many, to what to wear, and on and on. Check it out and also look at her awesome pictures. *www.tsteinkolk.com* or 212-706-7062.

Dave Cross has been a professional photographer in New York for over twenty years. After pursuing a career as an actor he decided to photograph actors instead of being one. In addition to shooting Broadway, soaps, movie performers and theatre companies, Cross' work has been seen in the *New York Times, Time-Out New York* and *Dance Magazine. www.davecrossphotography.com* or 212-279-6691.

Even though actor/photographer/writer/director Nick Coleman

is still working successfully as an actor in film, television, theatre and independent film, he's found time to carve out a successful career as a photographer. His graphic designs and artwork can be seen on book covers, theatrical posters, television ads, and as web graphics on internet sites and email blasts.

His webpage lays out all the fees and is a wealth of information beyond that. I particularly like his actors' jumpstart link. I think it's his actor-director-writer background that gives him the consciousness to ask all the right questions. *www.colemanphotographix.com or* 917-447-8057.

Jinsey Dauk started shooting pictures in the 8th grade. She studied and then taught photography at Wake Forest University in Winston-Salem, North Carolina. She also studied film production and psychiatry. Dauk is also a working actress and model.

Her webpage is worth a look at *www.jinsey.com.* There's a discount for checking out her work online instead of in her apartment/studio, so although that goes against my advice to meet the photographer first, it's worth $200 off the price. In addition to prices and packages, her webpage has a ton of other information that will be helpful no matter which photographer you choose. 212-243-0652.

SAG-AFTRA forbids an agent to suggest teachers, photographers, etc. (the union wants to avoid agent/photographer kickback at the expense of the actor), but some larger agencies have negotiated group discounts for their clients for webspace, pictures and classes. Because of SAG-AFTRA's concerns, if you ask an agent for a recommendation for classes and photographers, they frequently hand you a list.

Resume

A resume is sent along with your 8x10 glossy or matte print. Your resume should be stapled to the back so that as you turn the picture over side to side, the resume is right side up. The buyers see hundreds of resumes every day, so make yours simple and easy to read. No weird fonts.

If you have the luxury of a long resume, pick and choose what to list. When prospective employers see too much writing, their eyes glaze over and they won't read anything, so be brief.

There is an example on the next page to use as a guide. Lead with your strongest credits. If you have done more commercials than anything else, list that as your first category; if you are a singer, list music. You may live in a market where theatre credits are taken very seriously. If this is so, even though you may have done more commercials, lead with theatre if you have anything credible to report. Adapt this example to meet your needs. If all you have done is college theatre, list that. This is more than someone else has done and it will give the buyer an idea of parts you can play. Note that you were master of ceremonies for your town's Pioneer Day Celebration. If you sang at The Lion's Club program, list that.

Accomplishments that might seem trivial to you could be important to someone else, particularly if you phrase it right. If you are truly beginning and have nothing on your resume, at least list your training and a physical description along with the names of your teachers. Younger actors aren't expected to have credits.

The most important thing on your resume is your name and your agent's phone number. If you don't have an agent, get voice mail for work calls as it's more professional and it's safer. Don't use your personal phone number.

How to Structure Your Resume

I know you are proud of it, but it's not necessary to list union affiliation on your resume. The names of directors you have worked with are important to note. If you were in a production of *A Streetcar Named Desire* and you played Blanche, by all means say so. If you were a neighbor, say that.

The CD or agent wants to know how green you are; if you have "carried" a show, that's important.

Misrepresenting your work is self-destructive. Not only can people check your credits online these days, but you risk running into the casting director for that show who will tell you that she doesn't recall casting you. Even worse, if you list large roles that you have never played, you may not be able to measure up to your reputation. Carrying a show is a much bigger deal than just having a nice part.

John Smith/212-555-4489

6'2" 200 lbs, blonde hair, blue eyes

Theatre

Jersey Boys. directed by Des McAnuff
Billy Elliot: the Musical. . . . . directed by Stephen Daldry

Film

Men in Black 3. . . . . directed by Ethan Cohen
Man on a Ledge. . . . . directed by Asger Leth
Mr. Popper's Penguins. . . . . directed by Sean Anders

Television

30 Rock. . . . . directed by Don Scardino
Boardwalk Empire. . . . . directed by Timothy Van Patten
The Good Wife. . . . . directed by Rod Holcolb

Training

Acting. . . . . Karen Ludwig, William Esper, Sam Schacht
Singing. . . . . Andrea Green, Maryann Chalis
Dance. . . . . Andy Blankenbuehler, Christopher Gattelli

Special Skills

guitar, horseback riding, martial arts, street performer, Irish, Spanish,
British, Cockney, & French dialect, broadsword, fencing, certified yoga
instructor, circus skills, etc.

Open Calls

Although Equity Open Calls are limited to members of Equity, in 1988 the National Labor Relations Board required that producers hold open calls for non-union actors. These auditions can be harrowing, with hundreds of actors signing up to audition for a small number of jobs.

✦ *I represent a woman who was interested in being in "Les Miz." She felt strongly that she wanted to play Cossette and although I have a twenty year relationship with the casting directors, they were disinclined to bring her in. I encouraged her to go to the open call, she did, and she got the job.*
Jim Wilhelm/DGRW

✦ *Actors' Equity surveyed 500 members and found that 47% had found jobs through open casting calls. In calls for chorus work, which has its own system, casting directors size up the hopefuls who show up and point to those who resemble the type they are seeking before holding auditions.*
Jennifer Kingson Bloom/New York Times[4]

Although some do get jobs in musicals through open calls, all concerned say it's an endurance contest.

✦ *It's not just wearing for the actors; the producers, directors, and casting executives also find it daunting. And only a hundred were given a chance to sing half a song and hoof a few steps. Vincent G. Liff, the casting director for "Big" and "Phantom of the Opera," who turned away no less than 250 women for "Big" alone, called the turnout frightening but said the system, while patience-trying, was valuable.*
"We have cast dozens and dozens of people through these calls," Mr. Liff said.
Jennifer Kingson Bloom/New York Times[5]

The most successful people in any business are smart, organized, and entrepreneurial, but almost no one starts out that way. It's like learning to walk: it takes a while before you can get your balance.

As you continue reading agents' remarks about what successful actors do, you will begin to develop an overview of the business that will help you in the process of representing yourself. It's essential to stay focused and specific, and to give up the natural urge to panic.

Bring the same creative problem-solving you use in preparing a scene to the business side of your career. You will not only be successful, you will begin to be more in control of your own destiny.

You're Only New Once

First impressions are indelible. That first day of school thing follows you for the rest of your life. How you behave on the first day of school is how your teachers will always think of you. No matter how great you are the second day, if you trip the first day, you're stuck with that. On the other hand, if you are a good guy that first day, you can sin many days thereafter and still get by on that good boy image.

If you have a meeting with a casting director and/or agent and aren't prepared, it's going to be hard to get another audition/meeting.

My young friend "John" recently tripped. After being in town three years studying at a local conservatory, he met an industry professional who began acting as a mentor, answering questions, inviting him to events. About that same time, John was invited to sign with a manager.

The IP validated the manager and encouraged John to sign. The actor was sent out on all the usual things for a non-union actor in his position: independent films, non-union commercials, plays, etc. Finally, after a couple of years with the manager, John got the lead in an independent film that would pay for his membership into Screen Actors Guild. He was overjoyed and his IP friend was pleased and impressed at his progress.

Though the movie kept getting pushed for weather reasons, the fact that John had booked it convinced the IP (who had still never seen John work) that John was "sufficiently far along" to be introduced to an agent. He asked John if he would like to be introduced to a successful mid-level agent.

Overjoyed, John counted the days until the meeting. Shortly after he returned home from the meeting, the IP called to ask how the meeting had gone. John said he thought he had done okay and that the agency seemed to like him; "but I stumbled a bit in the monologue and I think the head of the agency might have noticed."

John was surprised when the IP told him that the agent had called the minute John left the office demanding to know why he had been recommended.

"I told you I had never seen his work, did he not do well?" the IP had inquired.

"He's a nice enough kid, but he was awful. He started the monologue and then just stood there at one point because he had forgotten it."

"Did he know he was going to have to do a monologue?"

"If he didn't have a monologue ready, he should have said so and asked to come back when he was more prepared."

Dumbfounded and embarrassed, John apologized to the IP. His mentor then proceeded to point out to John all the positive things to be learned from this unfortunate event. And although he blew this one opportunity, he now has valuable information:

- He didn't have a clear idea of what's a good audition and what's a bad one.
- He didn't read accurately how he was being perceived.
- He should suggest a return visit if he's not prepared. A simple: "I'm sorry, I didn't know I would be asked to do a monologue today, I don't want to waste your time unless I can do my best, may I come back?"
- He needs to commit to a high quality acting class, not the string of casting director showcases he's been involved in.
- He needs the help of that teacher evaluating any monologues the actor intends to show as examples of his work.
- He needs to prepare for every eventuality.
- He is not as far along as he thought.

Even More to Learn

If you can step back from the actor's point of view to the other side of the desk, there is something else valuable to learn. What if the IP in our story were an agent and had a Breakdown on his desk for which the actor was perfect. If he had expended his credibility to get the actor an audition and *then* the actor was unprepared? Then that agent put his own taste and credibility into question and the casting director might be wary of taking future suggestions.

This is why agents are only interested in meeting an actor who has either been referred or whose work he has seen.

If you really digest that information, it will be easier for you to persevere in being your own agent. Getting yourself work in plays or independent films not only builds your body of work, but also builds your experience in the audition room.

Acting is about so many things that are not acting. In this situation, John allowed himself to look bad because he didn't perceive that he had a choice. The agent asked for a monologue and John never stopped to think that he hadn't worked on that material for a long time. It never occurred to him to ask to come back. These are the things we learn over time. It's part of the "becoming" process of becoming an actor.

An actor who wants to be successful should have a monologue in his head, and a picture, resume and reel in his bag. You may only be new once, but you don't have to make the same mistake twice.

✦ *When I teach workshops, I notice that many young actors only want to get the agent and get the job and have an instant career. They want instant success before developing themselves and their craft. I tell all young actors: get in therapy, get into NYU, Yale, Juilliard, one of the League Schools.*
Jim Flynn/Jim Flynn, Inc.

✦ *Get decent headshots and a well-presented resume. Get "Back Stage" and look for showcase work and whatever auditions you feel you are right for. Go to shows, movies, watch TV so that you know what's out there and what is current. Get a phone machine that works and get into the habit of checking your messages.*
Dianne Busch/Leading Artists, Inc.

✦ *I think the philosophical basis is to work as much as possible, because the more you work, the more people have an opportunity to respond to it. Everyone in this business who is not an actor makes his living by recognizing talented actors.*

The smartest thing a young playwright can do is to get to know a good, young, talented actor so that when there is a showcase of the playwright's play, he can recommend the actor. That's going to make his play look better.

There are a number of stage directors in New York that, all they can really do (to be candid), is read a script and cast well and then stay out of the way. That can often be all you need.

Casting directors, agents, playwrights, directors, even stage managers are going to remember good actors. If they want to get ahead in their business, the more they remember good actors, the better off they're gonna be. Having your work out there is the crucial thing.

Studying is important because it keeps you ready. Nobody is going to give you six weeks to get your instrument ready. It's "here's the audition; do it now," so I believe in showcases. Actors tend to be too linear in their thinking. They think, "okay. I did this showcase and no agent came and nobody asked me to come to their office so it was a complete waste of time."

Well, I don't believe that. First of all, even a bad production is going to teach a young actor a lot of important things. Second of all, generally, if you do a good job in a play, it produces another job. Often it's in another showcase. Often, it's a year later, so if you're looking for direct links, you never see them.

What tends to happen is somebody calls you up and says, "I saw you in that show and you were terrific and would you like to come do this show?" It's like out of the blue, and it can take a long time. You may have to do eight great showcases or readings, but if your work is out there, there is an opportunity for people to get excited and if it isn't out there, then that opportunity doesn't exist. It doesn't matter how terrific you are in the office and how charming you are. None of that matters.

Tim Angle/Manager/Shelter Entertainment/Los Angeles

Show business is hard. Unless you are able to remain extremely focused and provide a personal life for yourself, you will have a difficult time dealing with the downs and ups of the lifestyle. Either get into therapy or start meditating; do whatever it takes to put your life in a healthy state.

If you are in an impossible relationship or if you have any kind of addiction problem, the business is only going to intensify it. Deal with these things first. If your life is in order, find a support group to help you keep it that way before you enter the fray.

People Who Need People

Life is easier with friends. Begin to build relationships with your peers. There are those who say you should build friendships with people who already have what you want. I understand that thinking, but it's not my idea of a good time.

It's a lot easier to live on a shoestring and/or deal with constant rejection if your friends are going through the same thing. If your friend is starring on a television show or is king of commercials and has plenty of money while you are scrambling to pay the rent, it is going to be harder to keep perspective about where you are in the process. It takes different people differing amounts of time to make the journey. Having friends who understand that will make it easier for all of you.

Ruth Gordon's seventy year career included an Oscar for acting (*Rosemary's Baby*), Writers Guild Awards and several Oscar nominations for scriptwriting *(Pat and Mike, Inside Daisy Clover,* etc.). In her interview with Paul Rosenfield she had words of wisdom for us all.

✦ *Life is getting through the moment. The philosopher William James, says to "cultivate the cheerful attitude." Now nobody had more trouble than he did except me. I had more trouble in my life than anybody. But your first big trouble can be a bonanza if you live through it. Get through the first trouble, you'll probably make it through the next one.*

Paul Rosenfield/*Los Angeles Times*[6]

If you don't know anyone, get into a class or explore one of the 12-Step Support Groups. There's comfort for every problem from Alcoholics Anonymous to the other AA: Artists Anonymous. Even though this group is for all different kinds of artists, you'll find a majority are actors and writers.

There are other As: NA (Narcotics Anonymous), ACA (Adult Children of Alcoholics), OA (Overeaters Anonymous), etc. No matter who you are, there is probably a group with which you can identify that will provide you with confidential support for free.

You'll be better served if you don't look to these groups for your social life. The As supply a forum where you can talk about what is bothering you, but these groups are not your family and, though helpful, they are not your best friends either.

Put energy into your personal relationships to fill those needs. You create your life. Will Rogers said, "people are about as happy as they want to be." I agree. I believe we all get what we really want.

If you are a member of SAG-AFTRA or Equity check out their support groups or join one of their committees. Being involved in a productive activity with your peers on a regular basis will give you a family and a focus – and might even lead to information about a job.

If you are fortunate and tenacious enough to find a job in the business, you'll find you are not only finally in the system, but you're also being paid to continue your education. There is no way in the world you can learn what it's really like to be in the business until you experience it firsthand. You'll get to spend every day with people who are interested in the same things you are. Who knows? You might not even like show business when you get a closer look. Better to find out now.

Get Into an Acting Class

In order to find a good teacher, you'll have to do some research. Who did he study with? What is the caliber of his students? Has this person worked professionally? You want someone whose advice is not theoretical. Work in class is totally different from actual professional work.

No one can teach you to act; a teacher can only stimulate your imagination and focus your work. Not everyone will be able to do that for you. Look for the teacher that will. Take the time to shop.

Teachers

If you are coaching for a particular part or audition, coaching one on one with a teacher can be a good idea if you can afford it. At a beginning stage of your career, however, it is important for you to interact with other actors so you can begin to practice one of the most important skills you'll ever need: the ability to get along with people both on and off stage. You'll also learn to evaluate the work of others and learn from their mistakes, as well as your own. Experiencing your peers tackling and solving the same problems you are facing will comfort you on many levels.

Here is a list of well-regarded teachers in New York. I know some personally and others were recommended by people whose judgment I trust.

JoAnna Beckson is one of the top ten coaches on both Disney Studios Acting Coaches List and The Actor's Studio Acting Coaches List. In Backstage's Poll of "Best of NYC", JoAnna was the only woman on the list of four. *www.joannabeckson.com* or 917-749-6922

William Esper is a widely respected acting teacher and director who has headed his own studio in NYC for over thirty-five years, and continues as director of the Professional Actor Training Programs at Mason Gross School of the Arts at Rutgers University.

A graduate of the Neighborhood Playhouse School of Theatre,

Esper trained as an actor and teacher with mentor Sanford Meisner, with whom he worked closely as a teacher and director for fifteen years. Esper's list of amazing credits is lengthy and includes a juicy list of students from William Hurt to John Malkovich. Find out more on his web page, *www.esperstudio.com* or call 212-904-1350 for information.

I studied with Herbert Berghof at *HB Studios* when I first came to New York. HB continues to be not only a rich resource for excellent teachers who are all working, but also offers classes that are extremely reasonable. You can check out prices online.

HB encourages you to audit many classes in order to find the teacher that is right for you. They offer classes seven days a week, during days and evenings. They define full-time study as seven classes per term. Until I checked the web page, I was unaware that HB offers a full array of classes and that full-time students can pursue classes six days a week and end up with a conservatory education. Whether you are looking for that or just a weekly acting, dance or musical class, HB is a respected place to study. Alumni lists are just a click away on their webpage, *www.hbstudio.org,* 212-675-2370.

Terry Shreiber Studios has an amazing staff including veteran *One Life to Live* director Peter Miner. Prices vary so check the website for information: *www.tschreiber.org* or 212-741-0209.

Karen Ludwig is not only an actress with an impressive resume, she writes, directs, produces. She teaches MFA actors at The New School for Drama in NYC. At Westbeth Center for the Arts, her class, "Word Is Out: Actors Write Their Own Stories for Solo Performance" is an ongoing favorite. She also teaches Intermediate-Advanced Scene Study at HB Studio.

Karen is one of the producers of *Uta Hagen's Acting Class/DVD*. Though no substitute for a class with Miss Hagen, it's still an amazing teaching tool. It's available at *www.amazon.com* for $39.95. Contact Karen at 212-243-7570 or *www.kpludwig@earthlink.net*.

Allan Miller lives in Los Angeles, but makes frequent trips to New York to teach. A member of The Actor's Studio, Allan is a wonderful actor, director, and teacher. Both his book *A Passion for Acting* and his videotape *Audition*, are excellent. *www.allanmiller.org* or 818-907-6262.

If I have mentioned a studio with many teachers, know that all teachers are not equal. Check to see who the students are and audit to find the teacher that seems right for you. See at least three for comparison. In a good class you'll learn as much about yourself and the marketplace as you will about acting.

If you're broke, see if you can work in exchange for tuition.

Dance Classes

Teachers with good reputations include Bam Bam, Drew, Soraya, Angel Feliciano and George Jones at Ripley Grier Studios, Rhapsody at Broadway Dance Center, and Kelly Peters at both Broadway Dance Center and at Steps. For more information check the webpages *www.ripleygrier.com*, *www.bwydance.com*, and *www.stepsnyc.com*. Many of the teachers teach at several studios.

Showcases

Showcases offer visibility, experience and the ability to hone the most important skill of all: getting along with people. But choose your material carefully. Playing *King Lear* may give you great satisfaction and stretch you as an actor, but it doesn't present you in a castable light for anything other than a Shakespearean company.

✦ *I think they should try to find a showcase which presents them in a castable light, in a role that's appropriate, and that is convenient for agents to get to.*

Before inviting agents, actors should try to get professional advice as to whether or not the project is worth inviting an agent to. You can engender hostility wasting an agent's evening if it's abominable.

Phil Adelman/The Gage Group

Be realistic in your expectations. You are probably not going to get an agent as a result of a showcase, but that director will direct another play or someone in the cast may recommend you for something else. You are growing, building your resume, maturing as an actor, and working your way into the system.

Analyzing the marketplace and using that information wisely can save you years of unfocused activity. If you were starting any other kind of business, you would expect to do extensive research to see if there was a need for the product you had decided to sell. In addition to checking out actors, note who is working and where, and keep a file on

CDs, producers, directors, and writers.

Note which writers are writing parts for people like you. Learn and practice remembering the names of everybody. Know who the critics are. Note those whose taste agrees with yours. Think of this educational process as your Ph.D.

If you want to be a force in the business, begin to think of yourself as one and assume your rightful place. Synonyms of the word force inspire me: energy, power, strength, vigor, vitality, impact, value, weight.

Take your opportunities to grow. Your weight grows with every play you see, read, rehearse, and perform. You absorb energy from every interaction, so put yourself with artists you respect.

The Unions

Beginning actors unduly focus on membership in the unions. Although routinely one-third of the 125,000 SAG-AFTRA members make no money at all in a given year (and the numbers in Equity are similar), actors feel that membership in the unions will change their lives.

It will. It will make you ineligible to work in both the non-union films that could give you footage for your reel, as well as the many non-union theatres across the land that would give you a chance to sharpen your acting tools.

Becoming a member of the union is a worthy goal. I can remember the thrill when I got my Equity card (somehow that was the card that meant you were an actor), but I was far along in my resume before I joined. It makes sense to wait.

Financial Core

While we are at it, let's discuss Financial Core, a situation whereby an actor resigns his SAG-AFTRA membership – essentially to play both ends against the middle – working both union and non-union jobs in order to cash in on reality television and non-union commercials.

I heard recently that a manager was recommending financial core to clients. That information caused me to review my history with the Screen Actors Guild and my own naivete when I first began my career years ago in Dallas, Texas – a non-union town at the time. I didn't know about any actor unions other than Actors Equity, and in my mind, I would become a *real* actor when I became a member of that union. But I was pretty sure I would have to go to New York to do that.

When I moved to New York years later, it was easier to establish a career in television commercials than onstage, so my parent union, and the one that made me a *real* actor, was Screen Actors Guild.

I was surprised to learn that as a SAG member, after earning a certain amount of money, I was entitled to medical coverage for my children and myself. That was just a nice plus, along with residuals, which were unheard of in non-union Dallas.

In addition, though totally unimportant to me at the time since the idea of my ever being older than thirty was not in my consciousness, I now had a pension fund. And if I were ever to actually age and become old enough to collect it, I would actually receive a monthly check.

Though union membership was pretty much a necessity in order to get good paying and respected work, the union was still an abstract thought to me. I appreciated the protection it offered when signing with an agent and the all important SAG minimum contracts with employers, but I never stopped to think what it cost to forge those contracts.

I'm amazed and respectful of those actors who put their careers on the line to form a union. Back in the thirties it was a different time and place; the prevailing thought was for the larger good instead of the individual. The union was originally formed to stand up to the powerful studios who controlled actors by signing them to long term contracts for very little money, and crushed the career of any actor who crossed them.

Can you imagine how hard the studios must have fought to keep the unions from forming? And how difficult it was to organize starving actors? You know how actors are; we'll work for free. I can't even imagine how difficult that journey must have been.

The union was formed to enhance actors' working conditions, compensation and benefits and to create a powerful unified voice on behalf of artists' rights. That's still the job of the union, but never was the union more in need of a unified membership than today. New technologies enable buyers to use our images without appropriate compensation, and management wants to keep it that way.

It's odd to me that someone (an agent or a manager) who says he works for the actor, who supposedly has the actor's best interests in mind, would ever advise an actor to choose financial core.

Agents and managers who urge actors to go financial core are short-sighted. If the actor needs to pay his rent, it's better to get a day job rather than scab the union. Each time a union actor crosses over into fi-core territory, he undermines his protections. The union is only as strong as its weakest link. The union is only able to demand decent wages and working conditions if all the professionals stand firm.

The term "quote" refers to the amount of money an actor will work for. We all start out at scale and after some luck and a few good roles, most move up the scale to "double scale" or whatever the agent has been able to negotiate for. The quote has been built over time when the actor was in a position to negotiate. Once you got paid $5000 a day or whatever you had been paid, that became your quote.

It used to be that when an actor established a quote, a CD might call and ask the actor's quote and then ask to see him. These days having a quote means less and less, as CDs routinely call and say "we're paying SAG-AFTRA scale + 10%, take it or leave it."

What if there were no SAG-AFTRA scale? What would that actor be paid then? I wonder if those who advocate fi-core would prefer to negotiate every single job that comes in and start from zero instead of the established scale SAG-AFTRA worked hard to establish?

If you want a career, intend to live in a house, drive a car and have a family, you'll find that pretty difficult to do without residuals, health coverage, and at least a minimum contract. You're not going to get that without union help.

For clarity, going financial core means you resign from the union so that you can work non-union work. The union will no longer let a member who has gone fi-core rejoin, but legally no one can keep you from working if someone wants to hire you. So the fi-core actor has his cake and eats it too. Moreover, he actually eats my cake too.

Anyone contemplating going fi-core should take a long hard look at why he chose to be an actor in the first place. I didn't know it at the time, but I became an actor to get a family. As time went by, I realized that the family created by my school plays was taking the place of the family I never had at home. Like many actors, I grew up feeling invisible and I appreciated finally being seen. I loved being in a play and being part of something, feeling like I counted, like people counted on me.

If you are a member of SAG-AFTRA, you do count; you are part of something. And people count on you.

Working as an Extra

While work as an extra gives you the opportunity to be on the set, unless you are looking for more extra work, I would not list it on the resume. You want any agent, producer, or casting director thinking of you for principal parts, so don't cloud his vision.

If you plan to be a career extra, working as an extra makes sense. If your goal is to play principal parts, why amass a resume that advertises you in a different capacity? It's tempting to accept extra work to qualify for guild membership, pay rent, keep insurance active or get on a set. I understand that.

I asked an agent if he had "John Smith" work as an extra, wouldn't casting directors and producers now only consider John to be an extra?

✦ *We all do. I spoke to a casting director the other day about an actor and that's exactly what she said. The actor has to learn where to draw the line and say, "okay, I can't do this anymore."*
Anonymous Agent

A lot of people can't. They get used to the money and the insurance and their resumes reflect that they are full-time extras. A credible agent might encourage actors to work as extras (after all, he is making a commission), but he expects them to know when to draw the line and stop doing extra work.

To me it's like saying, "here, these drugs will make you feel better. Just take them for a while, I know you will be able to stop in time." If you are not ready to get work as a principal on a regular basis, it may not be time for you to be in the union.

It would be more advantageous for you to work in some other capacity in order to pay your rent or to observe the business from the inside. Become an assistant or work in production. You will see what goes on, make some money and you won't be fooling yourself into thinking you are really acting. You will be more driven to pursue work that will further your career.

SAG-AFTRA and Equity both have financial assistance available to members in emergency situations. If you are not a member of a union, ask your acting teacher for advice.

There are also many city agencies equipped to deal with people in need. Low-cost counseling is available through both the city of New York and the schools of psychology of some universities. Call the schools or look online. A good start is The New York Counseling Center, *www.nypcc.org.*

Invaluable Actor Resources

Backstage (both *East* and *West*) and *Call Sheet* (formerly *Ross Reports Television & Film*) still print hard copy editions of their newspapers, but online subscriptions make the most sense because of the ability to instantly submit for the auditions they list regularly. Their online presence has grown as they became part of the family of showbusiness publications anchored by *The Hollywood Reporter*. In addition to their websites (*www.backstage.com* and *www.callsheet.com*) they list important casting info on Twitter. *www.twitter.com/castingnyc*

Backstage and *Call Sheet* are both rich sources of information for any actor who wants to take control of his career. The depth of casting notices available even without a subscription is pretty amazing. There is so much to digest about their resources that you'll need to visit their websites to begin to appreciate the opportunities. Although there is lots of free information, some info is available to subscribers only. Subscribing looks to me like a good business investment although some information (list of agents, casting directors, etc.) is available free online if you just spend the time.

Though many agents and managers advise clients to use these papers as information sources, they say trying to get a casting director to come see you from an ad placed there is not money well spent. They feel the prices are exorbitant and that it's unlikely that a casting director is going to view work from an ad in anything but *Variety* or *Hollywood Reporter*. Visit *www.backstage.com* or *www.callsheeet.com* or find hard copies at news stands or libraries.

These publications warn you that their listings are not verified. They don't vouch for the integrity of the people who invite you to audition. So use good sense and don't go to weird addresses in the dead of night. We've all read stories about actors, usually beautiful women, lured to their deaths by vague promises of jobs and/or connections. It's tempting to go to a producer or director's home to read for something, but make sure these guys and their auditions are on the level before you set out. Be alert for anything iffy and particularly those things that sound too good to be true. Don't go.

The Internet Movie Database (*www.imdb.com*) and The Broadway Internet Data Base (*www.ibdb.com*) are databases for New York casting directors, agents, producers, and anyone else looking for actors.

Actors Access (*www.actorsaccess.com*) is a free service for actors allowing them to post two pictures, resumes, contact information and (for a price) video links. In addition to this service, the actor has access to casting information and electronic self-submission via The Breakdown Services (*www.breakdownservices.com*).

The jobs posted are typically non-union, or very small parts or a "when all else fails" plea that a casting director might release for general viewing. These Breakdowns cover the entire country and are probably particularly more valuable for actors outside the large entertainment centers. *www.actorsaccess.com* and *www.breakdownservices.com*.

There are fees for each submission on Actors Access and each download of sides from Showfax. An annual membership fee gives you unlimited submissions and sides.

These two resources cover the entire United States as well as Vancouver and Toronto. Check them out online at *www.actorsaccess.com* and *www.showfax.com*. I'd try the service for a while, paying each time until you establish this is something that works for you. You should find at least one job if you use these tools intelligently.

Showbusiness Weekly, the "original casting weekly for stage and screen" was created in 1941. *SW* also has an online presence, offering many of the same services as Actors Access. Check online for current subscription rates. *www.showbusinessweekly.com*.

Casting Websites

There are many websites where actors can upload their reels and publish their resume. The trick is to find the sites that buyers visit:

✦ *Three of my clients booked a Bollywood feature film recently from choreographers seeing their work at* www.sceneinteractive.com. *Actors and dancers can put up their reels online on this website and casting directors from all over the world see their work and directly book them.*

Thomas Scott/DDO Artists Agency

At the beginning of my career I was fortunate to get a part in what turned out to be an important film called *A Touch of Class*. The night I arrived in Marbella, Spain, where the film was shot, I found myself standing next to the wife of the writer-producer-director at a party honoring the cast.

Making conversation, and truly delighted to be involved with such a lovely script (Mel Frank eventually won an Oscar for it), I said to Ann Frank, "what a wonderful script. Is this Mel's first script?"

What did I know? I thought he was primarily a director and, as a New York actress, I was ignorant of things Hollywood. Ann was so cool. She neither walked away nor behaved in any way condescending. She just began patiently enumerating the edited version of her husband's incomparable credits.

It turned out that Mel was a famous Hollywood writer, who with partner Norman Panama, had written the Bing Crosby-Bob Hope *Road* pictures plus many other classic films. I almost died of embarrassment, but Ann was all class. She patted my arm and smiled, "this will be our little secret." All the time I was apologizing for my ignorance, I was promising myself that I would never be in that position again.

If you have Internet access, it's a snap to power up *www.imdb.com* (internet movie database) or *www.ibdb.com* (internet Broadway database) to check credits.

I also recommend your library be stocked with books that tell you what the business is really like (*Adventures in the Screen Trade, The Season, Final Cut,* etc.), as well as biographies of successful people of every kind that will provide role models in your quest for achievement.

Many of these books are older, but I've not found any new ones that told the stories as well. Some give you real guidance about what a career costs and illustrate that success doesn't fix you. It may feel better for a while, but you're always you, just with a different set of problems. The more you read about people's journeys, the more perspective you gain. Here is a list of books, CDs and DVDs that will give your library a good start:

Aaron Spelling: A Primetime Life/Aaron Spelling
Act Right/Erin Gray & Mara Purl

Adventures in the Screen Trade/William Goldman
A Passion for Acting/Allan Miller
Audition/Michael Shurtleff
Book on Acting/Stephen Book
Born Standing Up: A Comic's Life/Steve Martin
Comic Insights: The Art of Stand-up Comedy/Franklyn Ajaye
The Devil's Candy/Julie Salamon
Equity Agency Regulations
Final Cut/Steven Bach
How I Made 100 Films in Hollywood and Never Lost a Dime/Roger Corman
How to Sell Yourself as an Actor/K Callan
Hype & Glory/William Goldman
Indecent Exposure/David McClintock
The Last Great Ride/Brandon Tartikoff
The Los Angeles Agent Book/K Callan
Making Movies/Sydney Lumet
Master Classes in the Michael Chekhov Technique/Michael Chekhov Association
Michael Chekhov: On Theatre and the Art of Acting/Mala Powers
Monster/John Gregory Dunne & Joan Didion
To the Actor/Michael Chekhov
My Lives/Roseanne
Rebel Without a Crew/Robert Rodriquez
Reel Power/Mark Litwak
SAG-AFTRA Magazine/SAG-AFTRA
Saturday Night Live/Doug Hall & Jeff Weingrad
The Season/William Goldman
TV Movies/Leonard Maltin
Ultimate Film Festival Survival Guide/Chris Gore
Wake Me When It's Funny/Garry Marshall
Wired/Bob Woodward

For inspiration, read Carol Burnett's *One More Time*, for fun, Tony Randall's book, *Which Reminds Me*. To gain insight on how to get into and what goes on at film festivals, read Chris Gore's *The Ultimate Film Festival Guide*. Roseanne's book, *My Lives,* speaks candidly of the behind-the-scenes intrigue involved with her show. It's instructive.

If you know of any books that should be on this list, let me know and I'll include them in subsequent editions. I consider books like *Wired, Indecent Exposure* and *Saturday Night Live* to be instructive and realistic about the business. I appreciate reminders of how easy it is to get caught up in the glamour, publicity, money, and power of this fairytale business. They keep my values in perspective.

Standardizing Non-Union Work for Dancers

Young dancers not yet eligible for SAG-AFTRA have a friend in the Dancers Alliance website, *www.dancersalliance.com.*

✦ *Welcome to Dancers' Alliance, an organization created by dancers to standardize non-union work. D.A. rates are minimums imposed by dancers and agents to protect dancers' wages and working conditions that are not covered by union jurisdiction. D.A. is not a union! These rates are most effective and attainable if dancers know them and make an effort to attain them on every job. You don't need to have representation to apply these rates to your work.*
www.dancersalliance.com

Breakdown Services

Back in the day, agents in Hollywood journeyed to each studio every day to read the latest script, make notes, and submit actors. Gary Marsh was one of those readers, doing the job for his agent mother. He changed the system forever when he called the studios and said something like, "if you give me all your scripts, I will summarize them and make a list of the types of actors needed for the parts, the size of each role, etc., and provide that information to all the agents. This will be better for everyone. You won't have those people in your offices and they won't have to drive." Thus Breakdown Services was born.

The much-maligned service costs agents and managers a hefty amount. Though they must agree not to show it to actors, some actors get their hands on it anyway.

Whether or not it's a good idea to have access to the Breakdown is debatable. Casting directors already don't have enough time to look at all the agents' submissions. How will they ever open all the actors' envelopes, much less, consider what's inside?

◆ *It's just plain counterproductive for the most part [when actors get their hands on the Breakdown]. The casting directors are likely ignoring submissions from non-*

represented actors. And as far as represented actors go, you better hope you're wasting your agents' office time pointing out what you're right for. Our work is about everything after (and hopefully before) the Breakdown. We continue to talk to casting and find out so much.

Often they want a name for a part, or are just looking for back-up ideas if their offer falls through, or change their mind about the "specs" after the first round of auditions, or cut the part, or a myriad of other factors.

Casting is an activity and that means change, give-and-take, and yes mistakes happen. For an actor to pin his expectations to the snapshot in time of a Breakdown is wrong. Our office's response to an actor quoting Breakdowns is "that's not a mail-order catalogue there."

Jay Kane/Talentworks New York

Whereas some actors are able to use the purloined information intelligently, others merely manage to alienate their agents. Though invaluable, the Breakdown doesn't include everything. Many roles aren't listed unless the casting director needs an unusual actor for a role.

Frequently the script is truly not available. More times than not, the audition sheet will be filled with producer requests, not from submissions.

Since not everything comes out in the Breakdown, it is important to assess your agent's other contacts. If your agent is not in a position to have more information than is in The Breakdown, that's still a lot of information if he uses it wisely.

Stumbling and Physics

You're not going to be perfect when you begin. It's part of the physics of life that you have to stumble a bit to find your way. My research of people and careers (including my own) leads me to conclude that there is a three year stumble rule, so don't give yourself a bad time for not having things together immediately. One just has to be green for a while before you can season and grow.

It's physics, a law of life.

So move in, get settled and begin your stumble.

Wrap Up

Tools for First Agent

✓ support group
✓ decent credits
✓ open calls
✓ audition DVD
✓ focus
✓ entrepreneurial skills
✓ integrity
✓ fellow actors
✓ growth – three year stumble
✓ marketable product

Personal Resources

✓ family
✓ teachers
✓ friends

Professional Resources

✓ job in business
✓ acting class/teachers
✓ theatrical publications

Reference Library

✓ educational
✓ inspirational
✓ indispensable

Breakdown Services

✓ important tool for agents
✓ can be self-destructive in the hands of the wrong actor

⊲ 5 ⊳

Self-Knowledge

Before you can sell yourself to the marketplace, you must identity what you have to offer. A reader e-mailed that she sent her picture and resume to many agents and though many asked to meet her, no one would sign her. I asked her to send me her picture. She was an adorable sunny Rachel McAdams type. I could understand why everyone had wanted to meet her.

I studied the pictures trying to figure out why all these agents passed after asking to meet her. I wondered what didn't match. Finally I asked if by chance she had an "edge," if she was more Angelina Jolie than Rachel McAdams? When she answered affirmatively, I knew we had identified the problem. All the agents who asked to see her obviously had room on their lists for Rachel but not for Angelina. Once the actress adjusted the picture to match her personality, a whole different group of agents responded and she was quickly signed.

✦ *[Actors need to] be aware of their strongest gift and concentrate on it.*
Diana Doussant/Leading Artists, Inc.

✦ *When an actor comes into our office, we only have what he tells us to go on, to teach us how to sell them. The headshot, the resume, the material the actor chooses for his showcase all tell us whether or not the actor knows what he has to sell. If the elements don't all line up, there is a disconnect and we can't sell that.*
Jed Abrahams/The Talent House

✦ *Before you start meeting people, you need to find an image to present. Check to see what the demand is and where you fit in.*
Ann Steele/Ann Steele Agency

✦ *Know yourself. You are the president of your company and you are the product. If you know what you've got, you can market the product better.*
Bill Timms/Peter Strain & Associates, Inc.

✦ *Be the best person you can be. Learn about yourself. You need a solid center to deal with life when things get tough. You have to know what your bottom line is and what you are willing to sacrifice in order to get what you want.*
Jack Menasche/Independent Artists Agency, Inc.

✦ *Be aware of where you fit into the marketplace and if you don't know now, you might one day. Most importantly, if there is anything else you can see yourself doing with your life, do it. This business is very tough and you have to want it more than anything else in your life in order to stick with it.*
Diana Doussant/Leading Artists, Inc.

Acting class is a good place to start the investigation into your persona. Ask your teacher to suggest some material for you. That choice will give you an idea how the teacher sees you. If you tackle a variety of characters, you'll soon get a feeling for the material that resonates within you. You'll see what begins to feel right. My first teacher, Herbert Berghof encouraged us to explore playwrights from our own part of the country.

Do you have the right talents?

When people use the word talent in relation to actors, they usually refer to acting talent, but other talents govern how effective the acting talent can be. Once you reach a certain level, all your competition is terrific. Any one actor sitting in the waiting room would be a good choice. The talent to self-motivate, focus, maintain balance and one's own voice under pressure will be the deciding factor in who prevails.

✦ *Talent has never been enough. Talent never will be enough. You have to have commitment and a singular purpose. Every decision has to be a career decision.*
Archer King/Archer King, Ltd.

When you hear about the thousands of starving actors vying for five agents and one part, you can screen out many of those thousands. They won't be your competition because they have no appetite for taking care of business. It doesn't matter if there are only five agents and one part, as long as you get the part and one of the agents.

I asked agents to name the most important single piece of advice they would like to give to actors. Almost everyone gave some version of the same answer, "know which one you are."

Don't expect to play Tilda Swinton's parts if you look like Kate Hudson. When I first arrived in New York, I did everything I could lest I be mistaken for the middle-class lady from Texas I was. I wanted to be a sophisticated New Yorker.

What I didn't realize, Texas accent not withstanding, was that my very middle-classness is what I had to sell. I have played women who went to Vassar, but more often buyers can and will get someone for those parts who actually went to Vassar.

I'm an authentic lady from Texas who has raised three children and had various life experiences that continue informing my persona. I'm a mother, a carpenter, a quilter, a theme partygiver, an ex-Catholic, a grandmother and on and on.

There is nobody else who has my particular components. If I don't prize what is uniquely me and find a way to tie that to a universality of the life experience, not only will I not work consistently and honestly, but my life will be a mess as well.

Also, as a person who has just begun to travel, I cannot say strongly enough how I wish I had started sooner. Traveling piques the curiosity and gives you a much broader life perspective.

H. Shep Pamplin has retired from agenting and now teaches and runs a theatre in Oklahoma, but he was a wise agent:

✦ *I personally believe that anyone who comes into this business has one point where they can enter the business: literally a skill, a qualification, that will get them a job tomorrow.*

If they are willing to take the time to find out what it is and go for that area, they can get hired, they can start working. And then they can begin to explore the other areas that they might not yet be prepared for.

There are certain qualifications that are required in every area. People who want to do musical theatre have to be able to sing and dance. They need to take the classes. They must do regional theatre and work their way up, just like in corporate America. Those who want to do film and TV, other than those soap beauties who land a job just on their looks, you have to have certain qualifications.

Whatever area you are strongest in, you should go for that first. Then when you are making money in the business, you interview better and you audition better. You meet people better when you are working in the business than when you are a waiter or a waitress trying to get just any job. You're going for film, you're going for commercials, you're going for television, and just grabbing for everything rather than learning to focus and say, "where can I get hired today?"

Once you are working in the business, then you can move your way through the path you want to be on. That's the client I like to work with. One that is already at this point and we can move you from here to here to here and take you to where you want to be. Then you are a goal-oriented career-driven client.

H. Shep Pamplin

✦ *Actors need to be in touch with who they are, their type, their strengths and weaknesses. They need an ability to grasp the fact that they can't be seen for everything in town and that just because a friend gets an appointment doesn't mean he will get one too. Actors have to figure out what they are right for and what they are best at; they need to know their own limitations.*

Gary Krasny/The Krasny Office

✦ *Know your place in the business. It's good to have goals and expectations but they must be realistic expectations.*

Bill Timms/Peter Strain & Associates, Inc.

✦ *Many young actors are celebrity wannabes. They're not process oriented. They're not working on their craft. They're not working on who they are and what they do and making that the best, bringing the life to it.*

They're more goal oriented and looking just to get the job. Unless you have the training, that one job you get is going to be a flash in the pan. After that, that actor's career is over unless they have a good solid foundation of training.

Jim Flynn/Jim Flynn, Inc.

Lionel Larner is out of the business now but he had a lot to say:

✦ *A lot of people are just totally unrealistic. They're either young and unattractive and/or overweight, and inexperienced. And they do have a chance of being an actor, but when you look like that, it's not going to happen for twenty or twenty-five years. They'll have to be a character person. They have a fantasy of acting and they haven't done anything about it. They must do the work, they must learn the craft.*

Lionel Larner

✦ *An actor can develop objectivity. It's very difficult. I don't know how one does it, but one has to have a certain objectivity about oneself and not freak out in certain situations that are difficult; in a crisis, not to allow your emotional life to carry you over into decisions that are not correct decisions. Decisions have to be weighed over a period of time and not in hysteria.*

Jeff Hunter/William Morris Endeavor

A friend of mine struggled when she first came to Los Angeles. I tried to help her by suggesting a part in a show I was doing. Mary was a young pretty actress with great comic gifts. The part was the town bad girl. She said, "you obviously don't know who I am. I have no breasts. No one will ever cast me in a part like that."

She wasn't whining, just stating a fact. When she got her break, it was playing an upper crust young lady born with a silver spoon in her mouth. The clarity with which she was able to see herself gave her a focus on and offstage that won her huge rewards. She became a hugely successful actress.

It's Your Machine

In an interview, Sigourney Weaver quoted George Wolfe's speech to graduates of NYU's Tisch School for the Arts.

✦ *He said early on he'd written this musical called "Paradise" and he'd had great hopes for it. And the day it opened was the day it closed. He looked out at all the students and said, "I'm going to tell you what your greatest teacher is, and the greatest creative tool you have in your career. It's failure. Failure will teach you all these things that you need to know."*

He said, "it's like standing in a huge casino and everyone has a slot-machine. And you're feeding your slot machine and nothing is happening and all around you people are hitting the jackpot and getting all this stuff. And you're going, 'well, I want to go over there to that machine. It's obviously a better machine than mine.' "But," he said, "stick with your own machine. It may take you longer. But when you hit, you're still yourself."

Scott Poudfit, *Back Stage West*[7]

✦ *Actors make a big mistake when they turn over their power to everybody else, making it about everybody else. Actors have to be very clear about who they are and what choices they are going to make when they go into auditions, and, if it's not working, to change their direction. You can't blame it on everybody else.*

Actors don't understand how the business works. I can't really blame them. All they want to do is act and everything seems to get in the way of doing their piece. I feel bad about that. They don't understand the reality of what it takes to mount a project, the amount of money involved, the fact that everybody involved is scared to death for their lives, their reputations, and that when somebody comes walking through the door, they better be less scared than these people are or they're not going to get the job. Nobody's going to trust them with the money and the responsibilities that go with some of the roles.

Marvin Starkman/Producer

Sometimes we do get the idea that insecurity is charming and that admitting it is even endearing. We announce to buyers at an audition that we are petrified of being there and that we are sure we won't do our best. Really? When had you planned to do your best? In front of 5,000 people? Will that be easier? Insecurity is not charming. It is not appealing. It is not endearing. And it is certainly not going to inspire the people with money to trust you with the responsibility of carrying their project.

If you find yourself in a continuing state of anxiety, there is either something physiologically wrong with you or you are getting off on it.

If you enjoy being a basket case, take responsibility for that. This can be a marketable attribute if you prepare yourself to play those kinds of roles. Otherwise, get yourself together and start behaving as though you have complete confidence in your abilities. Pretty soon, you won't be pretending anymore.

All we have is now. If you are not fulfilled by the now, get out of the business. If the payoff for you is the big bucks, the Tony, the Oscar or the Emmy, change jobs now. You will miss your whole life waiting for the prize. If you are unlucky enough to get the prize with this mindset, you will find you are just the same unhappy person that you were the day before, but now you have an Oscar.

Mental health, balance and self-esteem are essential.

✦ *An actor is in a very tough position because he has to believe in himself in order to produce. On the other hand, there's a point where an actor believes so much in himself that he's unrealistic. There's a dichotomy between self-confidence and self-infatuation.*

Jeff Hunter/William Morris Endeavor

The late Barry Douglas from DGRW was articulate in his analysis of the actor's self-confidence.

✦ *The most important person to like you is the audience. Before the audience can like you, the producer has to agree to pay your salary. Before the producer agrees to pay your salary, the director has to agree to work with you.*

Before the director can agree to work with you, odds are, the casting director has to bring you in and say you're right for the role. Before the casting director can say you're right for the role, an agent has to submit you. Before any of these people get to see you, the first person who has to say, "I'm good," is the actor.

You've got to be confident enough to take a risk with a piece of material, to look at a piece and say, "ah, I can expose the humanity of this character; I can develop the creativity of this moment of the theatre or film or television better than anyone in the universe. I am the first person on this." If the actor doesn't believe that, no one else will. It's got to come from the actor first. The actor who is too insecure to ask for an agent just might not make it.

Barry Douglas

Reality

In a fantasy business, it's a constant struggle to maintain perspective and remain excruciatingly realistic. You must realize that everybody's career is different. Someone may be twenty-five years old and be a star and then another actor may not make a dime until they are fifty. It's a sign of maturity to be able to enjoy the process and not be concerned with other people's idea of success. So your friend is working at Long Wharf and you're doing off-Broadway, everybody's career is different.

✦ *It's a business of survival. Your turn will come if you're good. It may not come as often as it should, but it'll come. They will eventually find you. You can make it if you can survive and you can only survive if you have no choice.*

Some go into the business saying, "Well, I'll do this for five years and I'll see what it's like or I'll do something else." If you have something else you can happily do, do it. It's only the people who are so committed, so desperate in some way that they'll put up with the humiliation, that they will allow themselves on ten minutes notice to be there, they'll allow themselves to be open and vulnerable; to still expose who they are and still be strong and protected enough to survive that kind of open wound life, they're the only ones who are going to make it, the people who have no choice.

Barry Douglas

Further in that *Back Stage West* interview Sigourney Weaver says:

✦ *You know, Meryl Streep was at school with me. And she was obviously ready for success more than nerdy me, at least. And it was hard, because she went right from Yale into Lincoln Center with no showcases at all. But I've learned that*

everyone has their own timetable and that's just the way it is. Everyone has their own path. It may not be the path you want, but in the end it's better for you.
Scott Poudfit, *Back Stage West*[8]

✦ *This is a business that rightfully or wrongfully, prefers prettier people. The prettier person gets the second look. It's a reflection of what the audience wants.*
Tim Angle/Manager/Shelter Entertainment/Los Angeles

The late Fifi Oscard had these words of wisdom:

✦ *I believe you will arrive at the success point you are intended to arrive at simply by working hard, not faltering, and having confidence that it does happen. It does happen. You get where you're supposed to get in our business.*
Fifi Oscard

✦ *Don't look at other actors' careers from the wrong end of the telescope. Don't look at what they did and think, "oh, they just went from one thing to the next. It was just this inevitable golden path and they just had to walk along it."*
Tim Angle/Manager/Shelter Entertainment/Los Angeles

Just because you don't get the job doesn't mean you're not good. There are variables you can't control. You can't expect any kind of time table as to when you can work. That is not the actor's life.

While you are paying your dues, you might get a job that gives you visibility and money for a month or even a year or two that makes you think you are further along in the process than you are.

Once your series (only one job, after all, no matter how long it lasts) or movie or play is over, you are not visible in that show business way and may think your career is over since your employment opportunities are no longer high profile.

Visibility is a double-edged sword. In television especially, the buyer may prefer a talented new face over an actor who has just finished a series. Frequently a semi-famous face finds itself unemployed because the buyer thinks it's too identifiable with a previous show.

Consistent Work

The task that takes more time than anything else is looking for and winning the work. Even two-time Academy Award winner Sally Field had her ups and downs. She says it isn't like she thought it would be. She's constantly reading scripts and creating opportunities for herself. When things weren't happening in films, she went to Broadway starring in *The Goat*. After her brilliant Emmy winning performances on ABC's *Brothers and Sisters*, she started reading all those scripts again and landed the role of Aunt May in *The Amazing Spiderman*.

That's depressing and comforting at the same time: If even Sally Field has to scramble, who am I to complain? I think sometimes that the most appealing part of the business may just be that the chase is never over. Maybe if they just gave me all the jobs, I might lose interest and leave the business. Yeah, right.

Assess Yourself & the Marketplace

Are you a young character person? A juvenile? Someone who is right for a soap? To see yourself clearly within the framework of the business, study the marketplace. View theatre, television, and film with distance. Notice what kinds of actors consistently work, not *which, but what kind*. What is common to the people that work? Who is like you and who isn't? Make a list of recent performances you realistically think you would have been right for. Ask your agent if he agrees.

As you become informed about the business, you will begin to perceive the essence of people and notice its role in the casting process. More important than the look is essence. The thing that is the same in the many diverse roles of Robert De Niro is the strength of spirit.

Practice thinking like a casting director. Identify the essence of various actors. Cast them in other people's roles. What if Tom Cruise had played George Clooney's role in *Up in the Air*? What if Kate Winslett had played Natalie Portman's role in *Black Swan*? Impossible? Yes, but this exercise will help you understand why you will never be cast in certain roles and why no one else should be cast in your parts — once you figure out what those parts are.

Does your appearance match your essence? As Tim Angle said, the business gravitates toward prettier people. Just as in life. Getting upset about that fact is like throwing a fit because the sun shines in your window every morning and wakes you up. Get a shade. If you are not pretty, be clever.

In dark moments I read Ruth Gordon's words from a *Los Angeles Times* interview:

✦ *Two things first. Beauty and courage. These are the two most admired things in life. Beauty is Vivien Leigh, Garbo; you fall down in front of them. You don't have it? Get courage. It's what we're all in awe of. It's the New York Mets saying, "we'll make our own luck." I got courage because I was five-foot-nothing and not showgirl-beautiful. Very few beauties are great actresses.*

Paul Rosenfield, *Los Angeles Times*[9]

The Process

✦ *Nobody changes the rules. What you can do is play the game for what you want or at least toward your ends. Nobody will force you to do work that you find insulting or demeaning. You have to figure out the rules in order to figure out how to play the game. You have to figure out what is a variable and what's not.*

If actors would take the time to put themselves in the shoes of the people they're dealing with, they would very quickly figure out what's reasonable and what's not. Actors don't understand why Equity Principal Auditions are a bad idea.

The reason is that no one can look at 250 people auditioning in a single day and give an accurate response. That's one of the reasons they only see forty people for a role. Knowing that isn't going to make your life easier, but it means it's not some arbitrary system where God touches this person and says, "you get to audition," and you, as the untouched person, sit there wondering. If you think about a director casting a play and you understand what he has to do to cast it as well as possible, at least you know what you're up against. It's not some vague, amorphous obstacle. It's not fair but at least it makes sense.

What you know is never as bad as your imagination. If you know what you're up against, it can be difficult, but at least it's concrete. What you don't know, your imagination turns into, "everyone in the business knows I shouldn't be doing this. I'm just not talented." It's like conspiracy theories.

Tim Angle/Manager/Shelter Entertainment/Los Angeles

When Sigourney Weaver was a young girl, her father ran NBC. When he left there and tried to start a fourth network, he received death threats and subsequently lost everything. Weaver says,

✦ *...From my father, I learned that business was not fair. I knew that things did not happen in any kind of logical, nice way. I didn't believe that people necessarily got what they deserved. Knowing that the business was unfair helped me.*

Scott Poudfit, *Back Stage West*[10]

✦ *We'd all be a lot better off if actors knew what went on behind the agent's door. There's not much mystery about what happens between the agent and the casting director and the director and the producer, as a lot of actors want to weave myths about. Most of the time, the actor is just not right for the part.*
Kenneth Kaplan/The Gersh Agency

✦ *Careers are like pyramids. You have to build a very solid base. It takes a long time to do it and then you work your way up. No single decision makes or breaks a career. I don't think actors are ever in a position where it's the fork in the road or the road not taken, where it's, "okay, your career is now irrevocably on this course. Too bad, you could have had that."*

If an actor looks at another person's career and says, "I don't want that," he doesn't have to have it. People do what they want to do. It's like people who are on soaps for twenty years. Well, it's a darn good job, pays you a lot of money and if you're really happy, great. But if you're an actor who doesn't want to do that, you won't. Nobody makes you sign a contract. Again. And again. And again.

Every decision you make is a risk because it's all collaborative and it can all stink. Every play at the Public is not a good play. Not every television series is a piece of junk. People make decisions based on what price they want to pay, because there is a price.

If you don't want to work in television, there's a price. If you want to work in television, there's a price. If you want to work in New York in theatre, there's a price. You have to decide if that's worth it; it's an individual decision, not a moral choice. It shouldn't be something you have to justify to anybody but yourself.

It's not about proving to your friends that you're an artist. It's about what's important to you at that moment. People can do two years on a soap and that can give them enough money to do five years of theatre. And that's pretty important. It depends on why you're doing it and what you're looking to get out of it. What is the big picture? Nobody knows it but you.
Tim Angle/Manager/Shelter Entertainment/Los Angeles

Jerry Kahn has retired now, but his words are still relevant:

✦ *One of the things I wish actors knew about was the business part of the business. A little bit more about their union rules and regulations so that every time you get an actor a job you don't have to explain to them what the contract entails. That information is as readily available to them as it is to the agent. It's irritating to have to go through all that when you book somebody.*
Jerry Kahn/Jerry Kahn, Inc.

Being Smart

Be circumspect with your comments about other people's work, auditions, casting directors, directors, agents, etc. It's hard to believe that what you say on your cell phone in the grocery store could get back to the wrong person, but just consider what you've heard on your last outing.

One of the most candid and entertaining people I ever met was the late agent Beverly Anderson who said her best advice is:

✦ *Be smart. Don't be naive. If you're not smart, it doesn't make any difference how much talent you have or how beautiful you are. You're dead. In all my experience of thirty-nine years, of all the people that I can sit here and say, "They made it," they did not make it because they were the most talented or the most beautiful or even the best organized or the most driven. They made it because they were basically extremely smart human beings.*

It has nothing to do with the best looks and the best talents, the best voice or the best tap-dancing ability. It's being smart. Donna Mills is smart. Alan Alda is smart. Johnny Carson is smart. Barbara Walters is smart. They made it because they're smart, not because of talent. Talent is just automatic in this business.

Who's to say that Barbra Streisand has the best voice in the world? I mean, let's face it, she sings well and has gorgeous styling and she makes a great sound, but who's to say if she has the best voice? I think the one ingredient that counts the most in this business is "smarts." You could be talented and be sucked in by some agent who signs you up and never sends you out and you sit there for five years and say, "well, I thought they were going to get me a job." Is that smart? To be smart is the best thing. Talent is a dime a dozen.

Beverly Anderson

Part of being smart is factoring in what your dream may cost. In an interview while working on *The X-Files*, *Californication* star David Duchovny underscored a reality I have witnessed firsthand.

✦ *"I'm OK, I can take care of myself, but I feel isolated and lonely. I'm not happy. If I knew what it was going to be like, would I have taken the series? Can I also know what it would have been like if I didn't take the series?*

I hate those kinds of things, where people say, "stop bitching, you could be working at Burger King now." As if those are the only two options for me, either act, or "would you like a soda with your fries?" But doing a television show is like

riding an elephant: it goes where it wants, with or without your say. Does that make
me an ungrateful bastard?"
Martha Frankel, *Movieline*[11]

Visionary Buckminster Fuller says it's a law of physics that if you
take all the wealth in the world and redistribute it equally, in a hundred
years (or fifty or whenever), the distribution will return to what it is
today. Some people work hard, some don't. Some save. Some
squander. Them that has, gets; them that don't, won't.

It's up to you and how smart you are: whether you make positive
choices; whether you choose to walk away at the first sign of negative
thinking; how well you know which one you are. You will have just
what you want.

Isn't that nice? It's all in your hands.

Wrap Up

Analyze

✓ how the business works
✓ who gets hired
✓ who hires and why
✓ which actor is getting your parts
✓ what do they have that you don't have
✓ your strengths
✓ your weaknesses

Important

✓ focus on the process not the goal
✓ study
✓ nourish your talent
✓ be organized
✓ acquire business skills
✓ be smart

♖ 6 ♖

Avenues of Opportunity

Now that you are settled, educated, and know which one you are, it's finally time to talk about agents. Many actors regularly curse and malign them, either feeling rejected that they can't get an agent to talk to them, or frustrated once they have an agent simply because of their unrealistic expectations.

You can save yourself a lot of heartache and ultimately move your career along faster, if you take the time and effort to learn how the business really works, how agents do their jobs, and how the agent is not the person who can make things happen for you.

Let's start by defining what an agent is and is not and what he does. Do you even need one at this point? Where would you find one? How can you get one to even meet with you and once there, what would you say? Are there rules of behavior? How can you tell if someone is a good agent? When is the right time to look for one? If they all want to sign you, how would you choose the right one? If no one wants to sign you, what will you tell your mother?

Unless your mother is an actress, she is never going to understand, so don't try. Those who have never pursued a job in show business (civilians and would-be actors who are still in school) can never understand what an actor goes through in pursuit of employment and/or an agent. So don't waste time on that conversation.

Just say: "Mom, I'm doing great. I'm unemployed right now and I don't have an agent, but that's part of the process. There are things I need to accomplish before it's time for me to look for an agent."

She's still not going to understand that, but it will mean something to her that you have a plan and it's something to say to her friends.

What Is An Agent?

Whether your agent fantasy includes the old-fashioned stereotype of cigar-chomping hustlers or the newer version of the cool customer in the expensive suit, many actors fantasize that the right agent holds the secret of success.

✦ Actors feel that if they make the right choice, the agent is somehow going to make them a star and help them be successful, or they're going to make the wrong choice and that's it. And that's just not it.

No agent can make anybody a star or make him a better actor than he is. Agents are only avenues of opportunity.

Joanna Ross/former William Morris agent

That being the case, what do these Avenues of Opportunity do? The dictionary has several definitions for the word agent. By combining a couple, I've come up with one that works for show business: A force acting in place of another, effecting a certain result by driving, inciting, or setting in motion.

In its simplest incarnation, the agent, acting on your behalf, sets in motion a series of events that result in your having a shot at a job. He gets you meetings, interviews, and auditions. And he prays that you will get the job or at the very least make him look good by being brilliant at your audition.

When an actor grouses that the agent is not getting him out, he seems to think the agent doesn't want him to work, completely forgetting that if the actor doesn't work, the agent cannot pay his rent. The actor also often overlooks the fact that his part of the partnership is to get the job.

It should be simple. After all, you've spent years perfecting your instrument, learning your craft, training your voice, strengthening your body, defining your personality, and building a resume that denotes credibility.

Haven't you?

An Agent Prepares

While you have been working on every aspect of your craft, the agent has spent his time getting to know the business. He's seen every play, television show, and film. He's watched actors, writers, directors, and producers birth their careers and grow. He's tracked people at every level of the business. He has networked, stayed visible, and communicated. He's made it his business to meet and develop relationships with casting directors, or CDs, as they are sometimes referred to throughout this book.

The agent you want only represents those actors whose work he personally knows. When he tells a casting director that an actor is perfect for the role and has the background for it, the casting director trusts his word. That's the way the agent builds credibility and it doesn't happen any faster than the building of the actor's resume.

In addition to getting the actor the right audition, the agent has to be prepared to negotiate a brilliant contract when the actor wins the job. That entails knowing all the rules and regulations of SAG-AFTRA and Actors' Equity, understanding the marketplace and knowing what others at similar career levels are getting for similar jobs.

He must have the courage, style and judgment to stand up to the buyers and must ask for appropriate money and billing for the actor without becoming grandiose and turning everyone off. The agent must also fight the temptation to sell the actor down the river in order to seal his own future relationships with the producer or casting director.

What Do Agents Think Their Job Is?

The Association of Talent Agents (ATA) is the official trade organization of talent agents. From their webpage is a description of their role in an artist's life:

✦ *Creating opportunities for their clients is at the heart of what ATA agents do. Licensed and regulated by state and local government agencies, ATA agents are at the focal point of change in the industry and at the forefront of the development of new relationships for their clients. In an era of media consolidation and vertical integration in the industry, ATA agents are the artists' strongest allies.*

In contrast to many other industry professionals, ATA agents are licensed and strictly regulated by state and local government agencies in California, New York and the other parts of the country where agents do business. In California, for example, ATA agents are not only licensed by the State Labor Commissioner and subject to annual review, but the artists' contracts are approved by the State Labor Commissioner. ATA agencies also work under negotiated agreements with DGA, WGA, AFTRA, Actors' Equity and AFM. While the SAG agreement expired in 2002, ATA agencies continue to work with actors under ATA state-approved agency contracts.

www.agentassociation.com/frontdoor/faq.cfm

✦ *I feel that I'm responsible for my clients' attitudes and for their self-confidence.*
Kenneth Kaplan/The Gersh Agency, Inc.

✦ *Sometimes actors don't really consider all the work an agent may do for them that doesn't result in an appointment. The agent may have said your name many times to the casting director until the CD has heard it often enough that he begins to think you are actually working.*

At that point, the actor happens to call the casting director himself and ends up with an appointment and subsequently a job. Now he calls his agent and says, "well, hey. I got the job myself. Why should I pay you commission?"

In my head, I'm going, "who sat down with you and told you how to dress? Who helped you select the photos you are using right now that got you that audition? Who helped you texture your resume? Who introduced you to the casting director? What makes you think you did that on your own?"

They don't see it. They don't see that, like a manager, I have taken them from here to there. I set up the auditions. Most actors don't realize the initial investment we make, the time, the energy, the phone calls, the mail, the hours of preparing the actor and getting them to the right places. There is no compensation for that until maybe two years down the road.

At that point, you've made them so good that someone else signs them anyway. There's not a lot of loyalty among actors. They'll always want the person who gets them the next job. They don't comprehend what we go through to get them ready for that point where they can get a job.
H. Shep Pamplin

Try to digest the truth of Shep's statement. It is an unusual person who arrives on the scene poised enough to handle himself in the audition room. That kind of poise usually cannot be acquired without going through the struggle time. An agent who invests his time and energy in the struggle time should be rewarded, not discarded.

✦ *If you sign someone, if you agree to be their agent, no matter how big the agency gets, you've agreed to be there for them and that's your responsibility.*
Kenneth Kaplan/The Gersh Agency, Inc.

✦ *I offer hard work and honesty and demand the same in return. If I'm breaking my ass to get you an audition, you better show up.*
Martin Gage/The Gage Group

Remember that your agent didn't sign on to be your therapist. One of the best agents I ever had wasn't willing to be my therapist. He did, however, initiate new business for me, was respected in the community, negotiated well, showed impeccable taste, and had access to everyone.

He also believed in me and retained that faith when I didn't win every audition. He gave me good notes on my performances, clued me in to mistakes I was making, and made a point of viewing my work at every opportunity and he returned my phone calls. That last item is a deal breaker as far as I am concerned.

A friend toiled for many years on a well-regarded series. She was happy to be working, but she was underpaid. She changed agents and doubled her salary. A year later she changed agents again: "They were good negotiators, but I couldn't stand talking to them."

You can't have everything.

Being a tough negotiator sometimes displaces graciousness. Your agent's job description isn't to be your friend, he's your business partner. You have to decide what you want and what you need.

Lynn Moore Oliver was still a Los Angeles agent when she offered a comprehensive picture of what agents are doing on our behalf, even when we can't tell they are even thinking about us.

◆ *I'm working on the belief that symbiotically we're going to build a career. While the actor isn't working, I'm paying for the phone, the stationery, the envelopes, the Breakdown Services (which is expensive), the rent, the overhead, stamps, all the things that one takes for granted in the normal turn of business.*

All this is coming out of my pocket working as an employment agent, because that is really what I am. The actor is making no investment in my promoting his career. If the career is promoted, we both benefit and I take my 10% commission. Meanwhile, the overhead goes on for months, sometimes years with no income. The first thing the actor is going to say is, "nothing's happening. My agent is not doing a good job." What they forget is that I have actually invested money in their career and I've probably invested more money in the actor's career than he has, on an annual basis.

Lynn Moore Oliver

If you think about what Lynn says, you will understand why credible agents choose clients carefully. Looking at your actor friends, are there any that you would be willing to put on your list and pay to promote?

Puts things in perspective, doesn't it?

Wrap Up

Agent

✓ a force acting in place of another, effecting a certain result by driving, inciting, or setting in motion

✓ licensed by the state and franchised by SAG-AFTRA

Agent's Job

✓ to get the actor meetings, interviews, auditions, and to negotiate salary and billing

⚐ 7 ⚐

Kinds of Representation

Now it's time to consider whether or not you are far enough to be signed exclusively to one agency, and/or whether it's even wise at this point to make that choice.

In New York at least, it's more than possible to have a career working freelance with several agents. Is that a good idea?

Freelance

If several agents want to submit you that might be a better choice at the beginning of your career, since not everyone sees you in the same way. One person might not think of you for a project while another would, so you might get in on more things. Might.

The drawback is, of course, that all this takes more time. Since you'll need to continue courting agents, making sure to see all of them regularly and remind them of your activities, much as if you were represented by a conglomerate.

The other downside (the one agents hate most) is that according to SAG-AFTRA rules, in order to submit a freelance actor's name for a project, the agent must clear the submission with the actor before his name can go on a submissions list. You've got to answer your phone at all times if an agent calls to ask if he can submit you. So if you don't, you could definitely miss out.

It's perfectly fine to freelance until you and the agent get a chance to know one another, but once you are an established actor, it's time to sign. I took too long signing myself, so I know.

If you are just beginning your career, target several agents and freelance with them until you get a feel for who you like. If you have the chance to sign, my advice is to go for it.

Commercial agents are more likely to work freelance than theatrical agents. Theatrical agents usually don't have the option of submitting a large number of actors for each role, so they're not going to want to squander their favors on someone who is not either a member of their agency family or plans to be one.

Exclusive Representation

A signed relationship with the right theatrical agent is a worthy goal. Don't be so afraid of making the right choice that you make no choice. Being signed can make your life a lot easier.

◆ *New York is much more of a signed town than it used to be. If you are going to have a career, you really should settle on someone because freelance is not the way to go. You don't get pushed. You don't get submitted for that many things and there is no development done, let alone any marketing.*
Gary Krasny/The Krasny Office

The agent makes his choice based on his belief that you will work and help him pay his rent if he submits you for the right projects. Once you and an agent choose each other, it is easier to stay in touch and become a family. It behooves you to put energy into the relationship so that the agent thinks of you. If you are signed and your agent doesn't, there are no other agents down the line to fall back on.

If you are smart, you won't give up your own agenting efforts just because you are signed. Instead, you'll focus them differently. Too many actors sign and sit back waiting for the agent to take over all the professional details of their lives. You and your agent are partners. Don't think that now all you have to do is act, you're still the major shareholder, so act like it and keep your antennae tuned for opportunities that you and your agent can cash in on.

Theatrical vs. Commercial Representation

Resume expectations of commercial agents are quite different than those of theatrical agents. Although this book is focused on agents who submit actors for theatre, film, and television, I would like to discuss one particular aspect of the commercial agent/actor relationship that relates to theatrical representation.

Some agencies have franchises with SAG-AFTRA that do not cover commercials. Some agencies have no franchises with SAG-AFTRA that cover actors for film and/or television. Some agents have everything.

Because commercials are more lucrative than theatre, some agents insist you sign a commercial contract also before they will submit you theatrically. If that is your offer, be wary. If they think they can get you work theatrically, they won't require commercial participation.

Frequently, the commercial resume builds more swiftly. The actor finds he hasn't had the work opportunities that lead to the same credibility and maturity on the theatrical level. He doesn't realize the agent doesn't feel comfortable sending him on theatrical calls because of the disparity between his theatrical and commercial resumes.

Paragraph 6/Gone?

Paragraph 6 of the Screen Actors Guild Agency Regulations allows either the actor or the agent to end the contract by a letter of termination if the actor has not worked for more than ninety-one days. The actor can void his contract with an agent simply by sending a letter to the agent plus copies to all unions advising them of Paragraph 6.

If you have been working commercially, but are not being sent out theatrically, you might want to find a new theatrical agent. However, since you have been making money in commercials, you cannot utilize Paragraph 6 to end your relationship.

On the other hand, if you have a successful theatrical career and no commercial representation and are interested in doing commercials, if your theatrical agent has commercial credibility and wants to sign you, why not allow him to make some realistic money by taking your commercial calls? Theatrical money is much harder to make than commercial money.

Evaluate your resume realistically. People win commercials because they are blessed with the commercial look of the moment. It's easy to get cocky when you are making big commercial money and conclude that you are further along in your career than you are.

What you really are is momentarily rich. Keep things in perspective. Budget your money and use it to take classes from the best teachers in town so that you can keep building your theatrical credibility.

It's possible to cultivate some theatrical casting directors on your own. A few are accessible. When you have done a prestigious showcase or managed to accumulate film through your own efforts with casting directors, theatrical agents will be more interested. It's all a process.

Signing Contracts

Carefully consider your commitment when you sign a contract. If you aren't making any money, it's tempting to sign with anyone who shows an interest. A commission of 10-15% or more of nothing doesn't seem like a big risk, but your stumbling around time will be over at some point and you will be making money.

That employment may be the result of an agent or manager working for you, but it may all come from your efforts. When you're making money, anyone with access is going to want a piece of it.

You may have heard about actors who got out of contracts easily, but I know actors who had to buy their way out for a lot of money.

Wrap Up

Freelance

✓ expands submission possibilities
✓ requires more upkeep
✓ requires vigilant phone monitoring
✓ gives you a chance to get to know the agent
✓ no overall game plan

Exclusive

✓ gives you more focused representation
✓ puts all your eggs in one basket
✓ allows a closer relationship
✓ it's easy to get lazy
✓ can backfire

Theatrical vs. Commercial Representation

✓ more financial rewards for commercial success
✓ all representation at same agency can block Paragraph 6 protection
✓ takes different credits for theatrical credibility

⊲ 8 ⊳

Research & Follow-through

Unfortunately, agents do not send out resumes in search of clients. Even if they are looking for clients (and they are all looking for the client who will make them wealthy and powerful beyond their dreams), agents don't send out a list of their training, accomplishments, and/or a personality profile.

Beyond their list of clients (which is not, by the way, posted on their door), there is no obvious key to their worth. Therefore, it is up to you to conduct an investigation of your possible business partners.

You have taken your first step: you bought this book. I've already done a lot of research for you by interviewing agents, asking about their background, looking at their client lists, interviewing some of their clients, and in general engaging in conversations with anyone and everyone in the business who might have something informed to say about theatrical agents. I've also read everything that I could get my hands on regarding their journeys and the way the business is conducted.

Agent Conversations

You should begin to have agent conversations with everyone you know. If you are just beginning in the business and your contacts are limited to your peers, they will probably be just as uninformed as you. Never mind, ask anyway. You never know where information lurks.

Ask what they have done thus far to attract an agent. Ask if they have a wishlist of agents they would like to have. Ask if they were able to get an agent to talk to them and why they picked that agent.

If you are in a group of actors and someone is further along than you and has an agent, ask that actor for advice.

Tell him you don't want to be a pest, but because you are just starting you want to educate yourself about agents and could he fill you in. Ask if he met with several agents first and what that was like, and if so, how he made his decision.

Find out how he approached the agent for the meeting, and how he knew to call that agent. It's okay to ask every dumb question you can think of, but first announce that you want advice, not help, that you are there to learn. Try not to salivate. Don't totally monopolize the person. Ask your questions and move on, thanking the person for his time.

How to Score

You can't make an informed decision about your readiness to attract an agent or what kind of agent you seek until you educate yourself. Learn how the business really works, what you have a right to expect from an agent, what you can realistically expect of an agent, and what your contribution is to the mix.

Prepare yourself as an artist and as a business person so that you can operate on the level to which you aspire. If your work and presentation are careless, what kind of agent is going to want you?

Before he agrees to meet with you, an agent has done his homework. He's researched you. If you had prior representation, he's asked about it. If you've done any work, he's called casting directors who cast you to find out what you're like.

He's going to expect that you've done the same. It's more difficult for you, but it's not impossible.

Get On With It/Agent Research

After you've digested this book completely, go back and read the agency listings again and take notes. You'll learn the agent's lineage, education, credits (clients), the size of his list, and have some idea of his style. If there is someone who interests you, check the index to see if the agent is quoted elsewhere in the book. Those quotations can give you additional clues about how the agent conducts business, views the world and how comfortable you might feel with him.

If you checked the agent's client list and don't recognize any of the names, that may just mean his clients are respected working actors whose names you don't happen to know or they could be up-and-coming actors who have not yet worked. You can only evaluate the agent accurately if you know exactly what his list means. If he only works freelance, that tells you something too.

If the only clients the agent has on his list are stars and you are just beginning, that agent is too far along for you. If the agent has bright-looking actors with no important credits, he is building his list. If you fit that client category, perhaps you and the agent can build credibility together. It's worth a shot.

If you are an actor of stature, you will be looking for an agent that lists some of your peers. There are always new young agencies that have opened in the last two or three years whose names may not be as well-known as older agencies, but who have real credibility. Usually the agents worked at larger offices, learned the business, groomed some clients and left the nest (frequently with some of the agency's choicest clients) to open their own agencies.

A subscription to *www.imdbpro.com* costs only $12.95 per month and gives you lists of agencies, clients and their staff. You can get a free two week trial to see if it works for you. Type in the agency name and you'll see a client list. It's not hugely accurate, but accurate enough for your purposes. Unfortunately, *www.ibdb.com* doesn't collect the same kind of information.

As your research continues, you'll have fantasies about the large conglomerate agencies. Check out Chapter Nine before you form your final opinion. There are many pros and cons to representation by star agencies at every level of one's career.

While you are salivating about life at William Morris Endeavor, consider that most stars come to celebrity agencies after they've achieved a level of stature and access that financially justified the interest of the conglomerate agency.

WME, CAA, UTA and ICM Partners do not offer career-building services. Although star representation enhances some careers, it is not true in all cases. In making your agent selections, make sure you are seeking an agent you have the credits to attract: George Clooney's agent is probably not going to be interested.

Make sure clients on the agent's list are your peers. It's all very well and good to think big, but you must walk before you run. Don't expect an agent who has spent years building his credibility to be interested in someone who just got off the bus. You must effectively agent yourself until you are at a point that a credible agent will give you a hearing.

I met a young actor with no credentials who arrived in California and managed to hustle a meeting with an agent far above him in stature. This was before we all had our reels on our computers and the agents wanted to see some film. Although he had none, the actor said his film was in New York and that he would send for it. He volunteered to do a scene in the agent's office and ended up getting signed – then he confessed there was no film.

A year and no jobs later the actor angrily left the agent in search of another, saying the agent didn't work for him. It didn't occur to the actor that the reason he had no jobs was because he was not ready for representation on that level. Not only that, once having landed the agent, the actor totally lost all the hustle that undoubtedly appealed to the agent. Instead of learning from the experience and rethinking his approach, he did what many actors do: he blamed the agent.

When you're in pain, it's tempting to lash out at whoever is closest, but the common element in all our problems is ourselves. The day I figured that out, I was depressed until I figured out the plus side: if my problems were caused by others, I was powerless, but if the problem was me? Hey, I can change me.

✦ *I feel sorry for the people who spend all their time trying to use various forms of manipulation to get an agent while their contemporaries are working and learning. And the ones working at working will rise right up. The people who were assuming it's some kind of game will disappear.*
Fifi Oscard

Who Do You Love?

At this point, you should have some idea of which agents appeal to you. Some names will keep coming up. Make a list. Even if you know you are only interested in Jim Wilheim or Jeanne Nicolosi, target at least five names. You can't intelligently make a choice unless you have something to compare. You don't know that you like Agent A best unless you have seen Agent B and Agent C.

It's time to ask advice from casting directors with whom you have formed relationships. A CD who has hired you will probably be pleased that you asked his opinion. Tell him you are agent shopping and that you would like to run a few names by him. Also ask for any names he might like to add to your list. Listen to the casting director's opinion, but remember that he has a far different relationship with an agent than you will have. Make your own decision.

At this point your research is based on style, stature, access, size of list, word of mouth, and fantasy. Let's forge ahead to face-to-face encounters.

Getting a Meeting

The best way to contact anyone is through a referral. If you know someone on the agent's list who will act as a go-between, this is good. If a casting director whose advice you have sought offers to call, this is better, but don't put the CD on the spot by asking her to recommend you. If you ask for advice about agents and she feels comfortable recommending you, she will. If she doesn't, be thankful for the advice.

If someone you contact just says, "use my name," that is a polite brush-off. Unless a call is made, the referral is useless. Anyone can call and say, "Francine Maisler told me to call." Unless Francine picks up the phone for you, it doesn't count.

What Can Get You in the Door?

Winning an Oscar, a Tony or an Emmy gets people on the phone. In the past I told the Young and Beautiful to drop a picture off looking as Y&B as possible. These days for security reasons most doors are locked and won't even crack an inch to receive a picture.

If you want to give it a shot and a door is opened to you, it can be a short-cut. It is sad for the rest of us, but true, if you are really Y&B and can speak at all, few will require that you do much more. Cash in on it.

Since Y&B doesn't linger long, if you are smart, you will study while cashing. You may want to work in those gray years of your thirties and beyond.

You're not Y&B? Me neither. If you are just starting in the business or don't have any strong credits, concentrate on classes. Join theatre groups. Get involved with showcases. View as much theatre, film and television as possible. Go backstage and congratulate all the actors afterwards even if you don't know them. If the writer and/or director is there and you liked the work, say so and give them your card and tell them you want to see the next thing they do and if they ever need help with ANYthing to give you a call. If you can find their email address, write the next day and invite them to tea.

This is not about getting a job, it's about building a place in the theatre fraternity.

Begin making a list of actors/writers/directors with whom you would like to work. Align yourself with peers whose work you respect. Form a group that includes all of the above and focus on furthering each other's careers by working together.

If all you do is get together in someone's living room once a week and read a writer's new work or a current or classic play, you have accomplished a lot. Write your own independent movie. I used the Kodak Z18 to shoot the little film now on youtube (just type in K Callan). It only cost about $200 and shoots in high resolution. There are complete movies that have been shot on iPhones.

Take a writing and/or directing seminar. You need to expand your horizons into those fields anyway. Make yourself available to read scripts or work in independent films. New York is the capital of the independent film movement.

Check out the film school at NYU and leave a picture and resume. Read the bulletin board. Volunteer to do anything that needs doing and you will gain access to the Spielbergs of tomorrow. Independent Feature Project (IFP) is also a good connection.

Don't approach actors or casting directors asking for meetings until you build up your resume and have something to show them. I spoke to an agent who told me that several young agent-shopping actors banded together and sent her a basket of goodies along with their 8x10s and resumes.

This definitely got the agent's attention. The downside was that the actors were still just too green to be looking for an agent. Don't blow your chances by getting people to look at you before you are ready.

I've always spoken ill of casting director workshops since I think most actors expect to be cast from these sessions. Even though the big signs say, "you will not get cast from this, the session is informational," the actor pays his money and crosses his fingers. I still tend to think CD workshops don't really pay off in jobs, but an agent I interviewed said he had a call from a CD who had seen three of his clients in a workshop and asked to meet them all. So, clearly I don't know anything about this. If you are marketable, then obviously it is a good idea.

If you are packaged and you are ready and you get a real casting director (not some assistant there to pick up $100 without any real power to cast) you could be cast.

It's a crap shoot, but it's worth trying. Somebody wins in craps.

Once You Are Ready

If you have graduated from one of the connected schools and/or have some decent credits, and/or an Audition DVD (see Glossary), and have a clear idea how you should be marketed, it's time to begin. Send a letter to a specific agent, not the name of the agency in general, preceding the picture and resume by a couple of days. This is not a cover letter. A cover letter accompanies material. Single letters get read; pictures and resumes tend to sit on the "whenever I get to it" stack.

Make sure your letter is written on good stationery. The feel of expensive paper makes an unconscious impression that the writer is to be taken seriously. Say who you are and why you are writing. State that you are interested in representation, that you are impressed with the agent's client list (mention somebody's name), and that your credits compare favorably. Mention any impressive credits.

I've provided an example below to stimulate your thinking.

Dear Mary Smith:

I've just moved to New York from Timbuktu and am interested in representation. I met George Brown and Sheila Jones in Karen Ludwig's acting class. They told me they have worked through you.

Since I am in their peer group, I thought I might fit in with your client list. Although I am new to town, I do have a few credits. I met John Casting Director and have worked two jobs through him: *Hello Everyone* and *It Pays to Study.*

The parts were small, but it was repeat business and everyone has to start somewhere. I'm compiling an audition tape. My picture and resume will be in your office by Thursday. I'll call on Friday to see if you have a few minutes and might be interested in meeting me. In the meantime, my reel and my picture and resume are online at *www.hopefulactor.com.* I'm looking forward to meeting you.

Sincerely,

Hopeful Actor

When you write to an agent, remember that on Mondays, there is a barrage of mail, so your picture might garner more interest arriving mid-week.

Make sure your picture and resume tell the truth and arrive when you promised them. If your letter has stirred interest, your picture will be opened immediately. Call the day after your picture arrives.

When you call (late afternoon is best), be dynamic and be brief. Be a person the agent wants to talk to. If he doesn't want a meeting, get over the disappointment and get on to the next agent on your list. Try to set up meetings with at least three agents and plan all the details of the meeting.

Be on time and look terrific. This is a job interview, after all. Choose clothing that makes you feel good and look successful and that suggests you take pride in yourself. Bright colors not only make people remember you, but they usually make you feel good too. Remember, in today's world packaging is at least as important as product.

Go in and be yourself. Be natural and forthright. Don't bad-mouth other agents. If you are leaving another agent, don't get into details. If the agent asks, just say it wasn't working out. Agents are all members of the same fraternity. Unless this agent is stealing you from someone else, he will be at least a little anxious about why you are leaving. If you bad-mouth another agent, the agent will wonder, subconsciously at least, what you will say about him. Not only that, it's not good for you to be indulging in negative energy.

In general, don't talk too much. Give yourself a chance to get comfortable. Adjust to the environment. Notice the surroundings. Comment on them. Talk about the weather. Talk about the stock market, the basketball game or the last play you saw. That's a great topic. It gives you each a chance to check out the other's taste. Don't just agree with him. Say what you think. If you hated it, say it just didn't work for you.

This is a first date. You are both trying to figure out if you want one another. If you've seen one of his clients in something and liked it, say so. Don't be afraid to ask questions, but use common sense. It's not what you say, it's how you say it.

Phrase questions in a positive vein. Discuss casting directors that you know and have worked for. Ask which CDs the office has ties with. Tell the agent your plans. Mention the kind of roles that you feel you are ready for and that you feel you have the credits to support. Ask his opinion. Are you on the same wavelength? Don't just send out; make sure you are also receiving.

Find out how the office works. If you are being interviewed by the owner and there are other agents, ask the owner if he will be representing you personally. Many owners are not involved in agenting on a day-to-day basis.

Check office policy about phone calls. Are you welcome to call? Does the agent want feedback after each audition? What's the protocol for dropping by? Will he consistently view your work? Will he consult with you before turning down work? Explore your feelings about these issues before the meeting.

If you need to speak to your agent on a regular basis, now's the time to say so. Does the office have a policy of regularly requesting audition material for their actors at least a day in advance of the audition? Let him know what you require to be at your best. If these conversations turn the agent off, better to find out now. This is the time to assess the chemistry between the two of you.

Make a mental note right now that you will read this chapter over again right before you go to meet an agent.

✦ *What makes a good agent? Partially the chemistry between an actor and the agent and partially the chemistry that goes on between the agent and the casting director; that they can communicate on an intelligent, non-whining wavelength. A good agent has to be able to not be so restricted by casting information and the Breakdown, so boxed in by what they read that they don't expand the possibilities. And finally, that they can get people appointments for good work.*
Marvin Starkman/Producer

During the meetings, be alert. There are intangible signs that reveal a person. Note how he treats his employees, if he really listens, his body language, how he is on the phone. How do you feel when he's speaking to you? What's the subtext?

The agent will want to know the CDs with whom you have relationships. Have this material available so that you can converse easily and intelligently. Even if your specialty is playing dumb blondes, your agent will feel more comfortable about making a commitment to a person who is going to be an informed business partner.

✦ *Morgan Fairchild came in, and out of the hundreds and hundreds of actresses and actors that I have seen and had appointments with, I've never been literally interviewed by an actress: "Okay, what have you done? Where are you going?" Incredible. She interviewed me. Yes, I was turned off to a degree, but I was so impressed by her brilliant mind and her smarts that I thought to myself, "Gal, even without me, you're going to go very far." She came in here and she knew where she was going and she interviewed me and I thought, "That's fantastic."*
Beverly Anderson

Beverly points out an important truth. Although she was turned off by Fairchild's approach, she saw the potential. If you want an agent to want you, it's like any other relationship, you can't be desperate. It's important to be respectful, but don't genuflect.

Tips for Meetings

1. If you haven't been hitting the gym, you've got a few months to shape up. Do it! In the short period of time you've got to perform, a physical impression will be as strong as any other you can make. Agents want their new clients to be appropriate for the roles that are out there, which are almost uniformly leading roles.

2. Unless you are another Kenneth Branagh, Shakespearian scenes are usually not as appropriate or as effective for an audience as contemporary material. Avoid Moliere, Chekov and other classics like the plague. Outside the context of the plays these scenes come off as dull.

3. Shorter is better in regard to scenes. Most people make up their minds about you in the first twenty or thirty seconds. Don't drag it out. No scene should be longer than two or three minutes.

4. Funny is better than anything, if you can handle comedy. Agents sit through a lot of scenes, laughter makes them grateful.

5. Try to avoid scenes that are done every year. The "Are You a Homosexual" scene from *Angels in America* is so overdone. There are other scenes in that play.

6. If you're going to do a scene from a film (which is fine) try to avoid scenes with are linked inextricably to certain performances. Doing John Travolta or Samuel L. Jackson from *Pulp Fiction,* or Brando from *On the Waterfront* is bad. Most actors aren't going to be able to compete with our memories of the original.

7. Dress simply but to flatter. Guys should wear jeans or slacks and t-shirts to show off their physique. Women should wear skirts or dresses and heels to do the same.

8. A showcase is NOT the time to explore your ethnic, racial, sexual or gender identity.

9. Don't do material just to shock or to talk about the inner you. More often than not it comes off as amateurish and polemic.

10. Finally, remember why you're there. It's not about art. It's about getting people to like you, to hire you, to sign you.

And a special tip from Jim Wilhelm at DGRW:

✦ *Make us feel something. Good acting has the power to make us laugh or make us cry. In two or three minutes, those are the buttons to push.*
Jim Wilhelm/DGRW

Closing the Meeting

Now that you have met the agent, focused on his accomplishments, office and personnel, impressed him with your straightforwardness, drive, punctuality, resume, appearance, and grasp of the business and your place within it, underscore that by knowing when it's time to leave. Sooner is better than later.

Make it clear that you are having such a good time you could stay all day, but you realize that he is busy and that you just have time to make your voice lesson. It doesn't matter where you are going. Just have a real appointment to go to and leave.

Suggest that you both think about the meeting for a day or two and set a definite time for when you will get back to him or vice-versa. If he asks if you are meeting other agents, be truthful.

If he's last on your list, mention that you need to go home and digest all the information. He will probably have to have a meeting with his staff before making a decision. Let him know you were pleased with the meeting. Even if it was not your finest moment or his, be gracious. After all, you both did your best.

My advice is to hurry home and write down all your feelings about the meeting and put them away for twenty-four hours. Then write your feelings down again and compare them. When I was interviewing agents for this book, I found I would have signed with almost any of them on the spot. They are all salesmen and they were all charming.

The next day I had more perspective. The hyperbole had drifted out of my head and I was able to discern more clearly what had gone on. If the agent said he would get in touch with you and he doesn't, leave it. There are others on your list. If he forgot you, do you want him as your agent? If he is rejecting you, don't insist he do it to your face. Remember, you are choosing an agent. The traits you look for in a pal are not necessarily the qualities you desire in an agent.

If you want an agent on a higher level who's not interested, don't be deterred. There are other agents on that level. If they all turn you down, then perhaps you are not as far along as you think. This just means you need to do more work on yourself until you are ready for those agents. If you feel you really must have representation at this time, you may need to pursue an agent on a lower level. But let's think positive.

Just like any other relationship, you're going to click with some and not with others. The agent is looking to see if there is a connection, if there isn't, there is a better agent for you and client for him.

✦ *When you have a meeting with an agent, make sure you touch base with everyone afterward. Send a thank you note or a card and, if you do decide to go with another agent, let them know how much you enjoyed meeting him and that you are appreciative of his time.*

Even if they say, "if you don't go with us, you don't need to call back," make the effort. If you treat people politely, you'll find that's the way people treat you.
Gary Krasny/The Krasny Office, Inc.

Making the Decision

Mike Nichols gave a speech to his actors one opening night:

✦ *Just go out there and have a good time. Don't let it worry you that the "New York Times" is out there, that every important media person in the world is watching you, that we've worked for days and weeks and months on this production, that the investors are going to lose their houses if it doesn't go well, that the writer will commit suicide and that it will be the end of your careers if you make one misstep. Just go out there and have a good time.*
Mike Nichols

I think that's the way many of us feel about choosing an agent. At the beginning of my career, I freelanced much longer than was career-appropriate because I was afraid of making a wrong decision that I was just sure could have irrevocable consequences on my career.

✦ *I find that actors are sometimes overly cautious. They are sometimes guided by anxiety or fear and that leads one to say, "No, I'm going to wait," when there is nothing to lose by signing with a particular agent who is interested.*

If it doesn't work, the actor can always get out of it. It's only for a year. There is so much more that can be done when there is an effective responsible agent at work that sometimes it's an actor's insecurity that holds him back, and I think wrongly so.

Gene Parseghian/Manager

There are some agents who don't share Gene's feelings. Many would rather not sign you if they feel you are not ready for a long-term commitment.

If you don't get in a position where you trust yourself and your instincts, how can you expect someone to hire you? How can you expect someone to put all his money and hard work on your judgments as an actor when you don't believe in yourself as a person?

Innovative's Alan Willig put it very well:

✦ *Know thyself and trust your agent.*

Wrap Up

Research

✓ peruse this book
✓ consult casting directors
✓ *www.imdbpro.com*
✓ don't underestimate word of mouth
✓ have face-to-face meetings

Tools to Set Up Meetings

✓ referrals
✓ good credits
✓ awards
✓ beauty
✓ audition DVDs

✓ a well-written note stating your credits
✓ picture and credible resume

The Meeting

✓ be punctual
✓ act intelligently
✓ be well-dressed
✓ be focused
✓ know what you want
✓ ask for what you want
✓ read this chapter right before you go, it will focus you

After the Meeting

✓ don't overstay your welcome, end the meeting
✓ set definite time for follow-up
✓ send a nice note

9

Star/Conglomerate Agencies

I guess we've all heard the joke about the actor who killed four people, ran over a baby, bombed a building, ran across the street into CAA and was never seen again. It's the quintessential actor story about the wisdom of being signed by a conglomerate agency.

It does seem like it would be nice to have the same agent as Brad Pitt and Angelina Jolie, but is that really a good choice for you?

The question is perplexing and research doesn't support a definitive answer. As in all other important decisions — who to marry, where to go to college, whether or not to have elective surgery, etc. — your decision must be based upon a combination of investigation and instinct.

Research leads to the conclusion that star agencies (CAA, UTA, WME, ICM Partners, etc.) have more information and, if they want to, the best likelihood of getting you in for meetings, auditions, and ultimately jobs.

A successful writer friend of mine was repped by one of the large conglomerates. She was making about $300,000 a year and an employer owed her money. She kept calling her agent asking him to pursue it.

The agent was becoming increasingly irritated with her calls. She finally left when the agent said, "I really wish you were more successful and made more money so I wouldn't have to keep having these conversations with you."

If $300,000 a year is not enough to get the attention of the big guys, then there are a lot of agents who will take your calls and treat you respectfully for a lot less.

What Do Casting Directors Think About Star Agencies?

I asked one casting director, "Who do you call first and why?" He answered, "CAA, UTA, WME, ICM Partners," and mentioned the name of a one-man office. The casting director said that although he can cast all the interesting parts from the conglomerates, he dare not skip this particular office because everyone on the list was special and capable of brilliance.

He explained that although many prestigious independent agents have hot new actors, the process is like shopping for a suit. If you want the best suit, you go to Bergdorf Goodman first. At Bloomingdale's you can get a beautiful suit and expect to spend a comparable amount of money, but Bergdorf has cachet, the perception that it is the source for the new and the unusual.

Casting directors also tell me they prefer dealing with distinguished independent agents like DGRW, The Gage Group, Cornerstone Talent, Nicolosi & Company and others and that an actor would be crazy to leave such caring families for a conglomerate.

But, since CAA, UTA, WME and ICM Partners have made it their business to represent all the creative elements of the business, casting executives and producers acknowledge that if they want to do business with star actors, writers, and directors, they will have to deal with the star agents and succumb to a certain amount of blackmail. "Take this one or you don't get that one," for example. So if they care, perhaps they could increase your employment possibilities.

It makes sense to choose an agency with a powerful client list, information, and stature. However, a well known actress friend has other thoughts. The actress works mostly in film, but had recently been doing more theater, an activity not prized by star agencies since relatively little money is involved.

She ended up leaving the agency. "It's too much trouble to keep up with all those agents. They won't all come and see your work. Who needs it?"

I asked if she would return to the conglomerate if she got hot. Her answer was illuminating: "I was hot when I was at the smaller agency. My name was on everybody's list. I didn't need to have a big office behind me. The only way I'd ever go back to a big agency is with a very strong manager. That way the manager could call and keep up with all those agents. So, no, I don't think it's necessarily a better business decision to be at a conglomerate."

It's true that the conglomerates have more power and information, but do those attributes compensate for lack of personal attention? The strength of the large agencies comes from having A-list stars. The bankable stars get the attention of the buyers and the agents.

Power Structure

When you have Andrew Garfield and Emma Stone on your list, you have the attention of the buyers. Of course, if you are Andrew or Emma, you don't need star agencies because you are the power. If you are not Andrew or Emma, you are filler.

A big star was in the final stages of closing a deal on a big new movie, when a higher-priced star at the same agency decided he was interested in the project. The original plans were shelved and the bigger paycheck did the movie.

An independent agent might do the same thing, but the chances are less likely that he will be representing you and your closest competitor.

Packaging

A large agency, one representing writers, directors, producers, and actors has a script written by one of its writers with a great part for one of its stars or first-billed actors. It then selects one of its directors and/or producers and calls ABC (or whomever) and says, "Our star writer has just written a terrific script for our star actress and our star director is interested. Are you?" ABC says, "Yes," and a package is sold.

Television pilots, TV movies and theatrical films are merchandised in this way. This phenomenon is called packaging. Non-star actors frequently choose agencies with package potential because they feel they too will get jobs out of the arrangement. The truth is that you can maybe package the first-billed actor and possibly the second actor, but at that point people at the studios and the networks want their creative input.

If you are cast in a project your agency packages, your agent is not allowed to charge commission because he is already getting a fat packaging fee. This can be a good deal since you won't have to pay commission, but it offers no incentive for your agent to place you in the package.

He cares much more about the packaging fee and doesn't care much who is cast in it. And if you are tied up in a job for which the agent is not collecting commission, he is unable to sell you for something on which he can make money.

There are many horror stories recounting star clients who were never told of an offer because the agent was withholding the star's services in order to get a packaging fee for the project. If the producers didn't go for it, the actor or writer or director never knew there had been an offer.

The value of packaging lays more importantly in the amount of access your agent is able to have with the buyers. Because the agent or someone at his company is talking to the buyers daily, there's naturally more of a feeling of comradeship.

Money Money Money Money

To the big agencies, it's about money. They have a big overhead. But actors have different needs. James Woods, interviewed by Stephen Rebello, spoke of a harrowing two years at CAA:

✦ *If there was anybody meant to star in a Tarantino movie, it's me. Ten days after I went with Toni Howard and Ed Limato at ICM, they sent me up to meet Tarantino. The first words out of his mouth were, "Finally, I get to meet James Woods".*

I'm sitting there thinking, "I haven't worked on a decent movie in two years and he's saying this?" I said, "What do you mean?" and he said, "I wrote Mr. So-and-So in "Reservoir Dogs" for you".

I don't want to say the exact role because the actor who played the role is really wonderful. I said, "Look, I've had a real bad year, so could you explain why you didn't offer it to me if you wrote it for me?" He said, "We made a cash offer five times."

Of course, it was for less money than my [former] agents wanted me to work for, but that's not the point. I wanted to cry. I'd rather work for a third of my salary and make "Reservoir Dogs". But I didn't get to do "Reservoir Dogs", didn't get to know Quentin, so I didn't get to do "True Romance" or "Pulp Fiction."

All because somebody else decided money was more important. They were treating me like I was an idiot. I made less money this year doing six movies than I made when I was at CAA doing two movies. And I couldn't be happier.
Stephen Rebello, *Movieline*[12]

♦ *The problem is that they're too big and they can't possibly function as effectively for an individual client as any number of not huge agencies. I don't see it, even for a star. I don't see the personal attention. To me, negotiation is easy. You keep saying no until you get what you want.*
Kenneth Kaplan/The Gersh Agency

Kenneth told me that when he was still an independent agent in New York. Since then, he has moved to The Gersh Agency, a bi-coastal agency with an important list of actors, writers, directors and below-the-line personnel. What does he say now?

♦ *Yeah. I know I said some things about conglomerate agencies in your last book. But I have to admit that being able to work from the script instead of the Breakdown, which is really somebody else's interpretation of what the script is, plus access to directors and producers, really does take a lot of frustration out of being an agent.*
Kenneth Kaplan/The Gersh Agency

There are many prestigious independent agencies that have had a shot at the big time and chose to go back to a more intimate way of doing business. One of my favorite agents has groomed several stars. When those actors became more successful and demanding, the agent grew tired of being awakened at midnight to endlessly discuss the next career move. It was disappointing when the actors went to WME or ICM Partners, but the agent just didn't see himself as a babysitter.

When Gene Parseghian was still at William Morris, he confessed that there were days when he wished he still had a small office with three or four people and twenty clients, tops. Gene is now a manager with a much smaller client list.

Jack Nicholson's agent, Sandy Bresler left William Morris and started his own office. When that got too big for him, he left and started his own smaller office again. Of course, he did take Nicholson with him. That helped.

Conglomerates are not equipped to handle actors who are not making a lot of money. They don't develop talent. They take you while you're hot and they drop you when you're not.

My friend was on a soap opera for ten years while her conglomerate agent collected 10%. When her character was written out, she went for an entire year without an audition until the agency finally dropped her.

Star agencies are interested in youth, not just for the longevity factor, but because the most lucrative jobs in television and film (the leads) are for young, good-looking actors. So if you have the look and manage to snag a nice part in a film that makes some money, you may well have the option of being signed by one of the big star agencies. If they are able to move your career forward quickly, you'll be well served. The conglomerates have access to not only the biggest star actors, but they also have the star writers and directors.

But if/when your career hits a snag and you have some downtime, as we've discussed before, the conglomerates have a very high overhead and they don't have time to nurture careers. They can move you forward while you have momentum. Once that's lost, you'll have to stoke it up again on your own.

A director friend declared that CAA was marvelous for him when he was hot with a new film, but when he let himself cool down by taking too long to make up his mind for his next project, the agents lost interest. Once he came up with a project to sell, CAA was terrific at promoting it and helping him realize his goal. He took responsibility for his part in cooling down and hasn't let it happen again.

Part of being a grown up and understanding how the business works is taking responsibility for dropping the ball and taking steps to get back in the game on your own.

For insights into the business in all areas, particularly into life at the star agencies, I heartily recommend Mark Litwak's book, *Reel Power*. All of us may dream of the validation we might feel as a CAA client but as James Woods said in the Rebello interview, sometimes that validation costs more than we might like to pay.

♦ *All CAA thinks about is the biggest salary you can get, period. My [former] agents were saying stuff like, "If you star in a movie with so-and-so, and it makes $100 million, then you can work with anybody." I said, "You know what? I beg to differ. I don't think that if you do a movie with Pauly Shore, with all due respect, Sydney Pollack is then going to hire you."*
Stephen Rebello, *Movieline*[13]

Manhattan Stars

CAA, WME, ICM Partners, Paradigm and Gersh continue to be the names on everyone's list of powerful conglomerates. Star wars continue between the powers as clients and agents defect and are seduced to change teams.

When Mike Ovitz headed CAA there was no question as to which agency was the most powerful. Today the landscape has changed so dramatically that you have to ask what kind of power you are looking for. Film? Television? Theatre?

Years ago my prestigious mid-level New York agent and I were talking about the disappointment of another mid-level agent who had really become a "farm team" for the major players. I said, "Well, what's to be done? It's true the smaller agent spent the developmental years and was more than a 10% part of making it happen."

He made a very good point. He said, "The client could easily make a deal with the star agency that the original agent would be compensated with 1% of the actor's future earnings. That would make all the difference in the world to the smaller agent."

So if you're ever in that position, think about rewarding the agent who helped you realize your potential.

When all is said and done, the swell offices, script libraries, limos, flowers, and packaging considered, you'll make your decision based on what is important to you.

I'm pretty loyal and I love my agent, so my vote would be for the prestigious, tasteful mid-level agency. But then, no one has plied me yet with limos and flowers, so who knows what I would do?

Wrap Up

Conglomerates

✓ have more information
✓ command more power
✓ have access to more perks
✓ can package effectively
✓ give less personal attention
✓ advice is corporate

✓ lose interest when you are not in demand
✓ have big rent; need big revenue

Distinguished, Smaller Agencies

✓ offer more respect
✓ offer more personal attention
✓ have more empathy
✓ might encourage riskier choices
✓ allow freedom for career fluctuations
✓ don't plie you with limos, candy or flowers
✓ less information
✓ less access

⚔ 10 ⚔

What Everybody Wants

If you could sign with any agent in town, who would you choose? Would WME be right for you? Could Bauman Redanty & Shaul be the answer? Maybe you would be better off with The Gersh Agency? These agencies are all prestigious, but that doesn't necessarily mean selecting A instead of B would be the wise career move. Before we look for the ultimate agent or agents, consider what agents are looking for.

The Definitive Client

✦ *I want to know either that they work and make a lot of money so I can support my office, or that the potential to make money is there. I am one of the people who goes for talent, so I do take people who are not big money-makers, because I am impressed by talent.*
Martin Gage/The Gage Group

I love the late Beverly Anderson's story about Sigourney Weaver:

✦ *She floated in and she did something no one had ever done. She had this big book with all her pictures from Bryn Mawr or Radcliffe of things she had done. She opened this book and she comes around and drapes herself over my shoulders from behind my chair and points to herself in these pictures. She was hovering over me and I thought, "No matter what happens with me, this woman is going to make it." There was determination and strength and self-confidence and positiveness.*
Beverly Anderson

Part of Weaver's strength comes from having a strong, successful father/role model, Pat Weaver, producer of *The Today Show*, and another valuable asset; a top-drawer education.

✦ *Come from a background of good solid training. I'm always attracted to the kids from the League Schools, from good theatre training.*
Bill Timms/Peter Strain & Associates, Inc.

One of New York's most insightful and successful agents, the late Michael Kingman, was articulate about what drew him to an actor:

✦ *His talent. To be moved. To laugh. Feelings. Somebody who has contagious emotions. I'm looking for actors with talent and health, mental health and the ability to say, "it's my career and I devote my life to this." It's an attitude, not a spoken thing. It's an attitude that says, "today is not the last day of my life."*
Michael Kingman

Geez, if we had mental health, would we need to be actors?

✦ *We're not afraid to do the heavy lifting when it comes to developing talent. Many companies are looking for your general leading man and woman and so are we, but we also look for and foster unique talents that may not fit in a particular mold. If we meet someone with tremendous talent and confidence, even though they are green in the business, we don't mind guiding them, suggesting teachers, formatting their resumes to the industry standard and making sure they get great pictures so their unique talents will get noticed by casting directors.*
Renee Glicker/About Artists Agency

✦ *We are always looking for young people age fifteen to twenty-five who are savvy about the biz and have poise and talent. Good looks are extremely important to our TV and film contacts, so we are forced to make that important too.*
Dianne Busch/Leading Artists, Inc.

✦ *The people we work with best are actors who are committed to their craft and are willing to do regional theatre as well as off-Broadway and Broadway as well as film and television. The focus should be on training and growing yourself.*
Experiencing life so you can bring that to a character and to a performance. The interview part of the audition is just as important as the audition. Who you are as a person, as well as who you are as an actor.
Jim Flynn/Jim Flynn, Inc.

✦ *It always boils down to the talent. If somebody has a talent even though it's someone who's a drunk, you know that there's still the wonderful performance to be gotten. On the other hand, you must ask, "Is it worth going through all that to wait for that wonderful performance?"*
Jeff Hunter/William Morris Endeavor

Actress Laurie Walton was an agent for a while. She said her perspective totally changed when she became an agent:

✦ *It's really difficult to turn down actors. Old friends need an agent. I want to help them all out, but when my boss holds that picture up in front of my face and says, "are you ready to make a phone call to Jay Binder and ask him to see this client?" That puts things more in perspective. And actors don't understand that I don't make the sole decision.*
Laurie Walton

✦ *I look for preparedness, humor – about the process of looking for work – thick-skin (unfortunately).*
Jay Kane/Talentworks New York.

✦ *The things that attract me are the sense of self as an actor, sense of humor, being prepared, taking responsibility for themselves and their work.*
Diana Doussant/Leading Artists, Inc.

✦ *I want clients to come to me prepared, to have a sense of who they are, the kind of career they're likely to have, good self-knowledge, good reality about themselves.*
Phil Adelman/The Gage Group

✦ *If they're older and have been in the business and don't have some career going, it's harder because they're now going to be up against people who have many more important credits.*
Robert Malcolm/The Artists Group

✦ *Since I am my own boss, I can choose who I want to work with. When a client approaches and I get even an inkling that this is going to be a high-maintenance client, I don't choose him.*
Jim Flynn/Jim Flynn, Inc.

✦ *Actors need to know themselves and what they have to sell. If you are a character actor, embrace it. Don't try to see yourself as the ingenue or the leading man if you're not. I've had actors come in telling me that they are very funny. Then, they sing a song to showcase their pretty voice instead of the comedic talent that will make them stars. I'll frequently tell an actor to go home and learn three new songs that showcase their comedy skills.*
Jed Abrahams/The Talent House

+ *I think it's important for an actor to be able to adjust to auditioning being their main job. Their goal has to be to do a great audition and then let it go. If they book the job, that's the cherry on top.*
Renee Glicker/About Artists Agency

+ *A spark. Something that's unusual. Usually from a performance. But they can cool my interest by their behavior at our interview. You not only have to have the talent, you have to apply it. You can tell sometimes by their responses that they don't yet have that capacity.*
Jeff Hunter/William Morris Endeavor

Notice what Jeff said. They don't *yet* have the capacity, that doesn't mean you're not going to. It doesn't even mean the agent thinks you're not going to. You just don't have it *yet*. Remember process.

What to Look for in an Agent

+ *Schools sometimes give students a laundry list of questions to ask agents that the actors ask without even knowing why they ask them. When I meet an actor, I want to have a conversation with him out of which questions come.*

I think actors should have an idea of what they want to hire because they are hiring the agent. If I were an actor, I'd want to know that the agent and I were on the same page about the kinds of projects he would be interested in submitting me for. I'd want to know the agent's perception of my ability.

The art of communication is extremely important. You have to imagine that apart from your lover, family, boyfriend, this is the person you are going to speak to more often than your mother and you have to not be intimidated to pick up the phone and have a conversation. Is that agent someone I want to talk to?
Jim Wilhelm/DGRW

Busy Work?

Be practical in your assessment of auditions. Actors sometime grade their agents by the number of auditions they generate, not the quality or appropriateness. If you're not being sent on projects that you are right for, all those auditions are just for show. Producer and former agent Marvin Starkman has a realistic perspective:

+ *If the actor/agent relationship were based on getting auditions for everything, then*

the agent would have a right to say that you must get everything he sends you out on. If you don't get everything he sends you on, then you have a one-sided relationship.
Marvin Starkman

Ouch! Of course, that's predicated on his getting you out on everything in town. But still, his point is well taken. Neither actor not agent is going to score every time.

Vision/Goals

The actor and agent need to be on the same wavelength:

✦ *I had a funny looking lady come in, mid thirties, chubby, not very pretty. For all I know, this woman could be brilliant. I asked her what roles she could play, what she thought she should get. She saw herself playing Gwyneth Paltrow's roles.*

I could have been potentially interested in this woman in the areas in which she could work. But it was a turnoff, because not only do I know that she's not going after the right things so she's not preparing correctly, but she's not going to be happy with the kinds of things I'm going to be able to do for her. So I wouldn't want to commit to that person.
Phil Adelman/The Gage Group

✦ *What's essential is that the goals the actor sets for himself and what the agent wants for the actor be the same. Or at the very least, compatible, but probably the same. If an actor walks in and I think that actor can be a star next month and the actor doesn't, it ain't gonna happen.*

If the actor thinks he's gonna be a star next month and I don't, it ain't gonna happen. By that, I mean it's not gonna work between us. Even though a great deal of it may be unspoken, there has to be a shared perspective.
Gene Parseghian/Parseghian Planco

Size

A key aspect to consider in overall agent effectiveness is size. When we speak of size in relation to agents, we are speaking of his client list: the number of actors the agent has committed to represent exclusively.

One person can't effectively represent a hundred people. It's like going to the store and buying everything you see. You can't possibly use it all, you're just taking it out of circulation. There are some agents who may sign you just to protect their client who is in your category.

It might feed your ego to be signed ("I have an agent!"), but if you are not signed with a credible agent that you can trust, you may just be taking yourself out of the marketplace.

Better to wait until you have the credits to support getting a better agent than to sign with someone who can't represent you effectively. Many agents believe a good ratio is one agent to twenty to twenty-five clients. An agency with four agents can do well by a hundred or even a hundred and forty clients, but that really is the limit.

Or it used to be the limit. More and more agencies are loading up their list with far more clients than they can handle. For one thing, even though the list might be full, it's hard to resist a promising talent.

Though I list the size of their lists in my book, many agents may say they have less clients than they do – because that looks better.

An agency with a lot of series regulars has clients who are out of circulation for a large part of the year and don't require much upkeep, which gives the agent time to attend to other clients. It's dicey. Bottom line is how much attention you find you are/are not getting.

It's easy to get lost on a large list. It's easy to get lost on a small list too. It all depends on if you can keep up their enthusiasm.

It's all very well to have stamina, discern talent, have a short list, and be a great salesman. I take that as a given. But there are two other attributes that separate the contenders from the also-rans.

Access and Stature

The dictionary defines the word access as "ability to approach" or "admittance." Since the conglomerate agencies have many stars on their lists, they have plenty of ability to approach. If the studios, networks, and producers do not return their phone calls, they might find the agency retaliating by withholding their important stars.

Stature on the other hand is different entirely. Webster defines the word as "level of achievement." Thus, Phil Adelman (The Gage Group) and Bruce Ostler (Bret Adams) certainly have more stature than some beginning agent at WME, but because Adelman and Bruce don't have an equal number of bankable stars, they might not have as much access. Get both stature and access if you can, but if you have to choose, go with access.

The central issue is, how do you choose the agent who will provide the opportunity for you to be gainfully employed in the business?

Wrap Up

The Ideal Client

✓ has talent
✓ possesses contagious emotions
✓ displays a singular personality
✓ exhibits professionalism
✓ manifests self-knowledge
✓ shows drive
✓ is innately likeable
✓ maintains mental health
✓ is well-trained
✓ boasts a good resume

The Ideal Agent/Manager

✓ is aggressive
✓ has stature
✓ has access
✓ is enthusiastic
✓ shares the actor's career vision
✓ has optimum actor/rep ratio
✓ has integrity

⚔ 11 ⚔

Everybody's Responsibilities

Once you have made a decision, there are many things to do. If you are switching agents, it's only right to have a face-to-face meeting to say goodbye. Say you're sorry it didn't work out and follow-up afterwards with a nice handwritten note saying the same thing. Make it a point to thank all your agents individually, as well as everyone else in the office. Then pick up your pictures, DVDs, etc. and leave. If the parting is amicable, buy your agent a drink if that's appropriate. You might want to send flowers. Send the necessary letters to the unions.

Please do the universe a favor and don't break up by e-mail. Have a little more class than that.

Setting Up Shop

The next stop is your new partner's office to sign contracts and meet and fix in your mind all the auxiliary people who will be working for you. Make notes as soon as you leave the office as to who is who and where they sit. Until you become more familiar with them, you can consult the map before subsequent visits.

Leave a supply of pictures, resumes and DVDs. Be sparing. Bringing supplies is always a good excuse for dropping by. Make a list for each agent's file of the casting directors, producers and directors with whom you have relationships.

Alphabetize them if you ever want them used. Also leave lists of your quotes (how much you were paid for your last jobs in theatre, film, and television), plus information about billing. The more background you give your agent, the better he can represent you.

Now the real work begins. Remember the agent only gets 10% of the money. You can't really expect him to do 100% of the work. That may be why you are leaving your old agent. You felt he didn't work hard enough. Maybe your expectations were out of line. Maybe you were lazy. Maybe you didn't keep his enthusiasm high enough. Maybe he was a goof-off. Even if that was the case before, it really doesn't matter now.

What matters now is how well you and your new agent are going to function together.

90%-10%

The concept of 90%-10% is fascinating. How many of us have resented our agents when we have been requested for a job and all the agent had to do was negotiate? In fact, if all our jobs were requests, would we just have a lawyer negotiate and do away with the agent altogether? Or is the support and feedback worth something?

Maybe our whole thought process about agents is incorrect. In our hearts we really think the agent is going to get us a job. Based upon my years in the business and my research, I finally know that the agent does not get me work. He gets my appointments, but my work gets me work. This happens not only by my ability to function well as an actress, but also by my adjustment to life.

The times I have not worked steadily have been directly connected to either physical or emotional growth spurts. I went into a terrible depression when my children left home. I willed myself to be up, but it was a loss that I had to mourn. I wasn't all that aware of it, but when your energy is depleted, you're not going to spark a room.

Life's processes must be endured. We can change agents, mates and clothes sizes, but we can't alter reality. We must experience it. Those realities are reflected in our work and ultimately enrich us as performers.

✦ *If you're not working because you are in your mid-life crisis, divorce, whatever, you may not be able to readily fix it, but it's up to you to assume you have a problem and set out to fix it.*
Martin Gage/The Gage Group

We can hope that agents are going to initiate work for us and introduce us to the casting directors, producers, directors, etc. What they are really going to do over the span of a career is negotiate, initiate meetings, arrange appointments when we are requested and hopefully, support us in dark moments and help us retain perspective in our bright ones. Notice I say moments. Neither state lasts as long as it seems.

Because we are getting 90% of the money, we have to give up being cranky when we have to do 90% of the work. I assume you are willing to do that, if you only knew what that meant.

What the Actor Can Do

✦ *The actor's job is to give me something I can sell: a showcase, a new picture, a wonderful credit with a tour de force role. He has to be president of his own company, to treat the agent as his employee, to motivate him, to help guide him and to find a way to communicate with him so they can work as a team.*
Nancy Curtis/Harden Curtis Associates

✦ *Trust me to have your interests at heart. Check you messages frequently. Live your life but let me know before you buy a ticket out of town. Keep up with what's happening. Always be as prepared as possible for your auditions.*
Dianne Busch/Leading Artists, Inc.

✦ *See everything you can, film, television, theatre. What's filming in New York? What's the style of it? See who they are hiring. If there is something in town that has a part for you, go see it. Sooner or later, they're going to need replacements.*
Bill Timms/Peter Strain & Associates, Inc.

Nancy Curtis envisions her advice to all clients written on her tombstone: *Run your own company.* Her partner, Mary Harden feels communication and a strong career plan are key to a successful actor-agent relationship.

✦ *Stay positive and make sure you look good, be part of the artistic community where information is passed around, and don't alienate your fellow artists.*
Diana Doussant/Leading Artists, Inc.

✦ *I like our clients to be pro-active and to stay in contact with the office. Let me know if you have a special relationship with a director who's casting his new production. Information is a powerful tool. Keep your resumes updated. Return calls promptly. Remember, this is a partnership: both actor and agent working in tandem to build a career.*
Jeanne Nicolosi/Nicolosi & Co., Inc.

✦ *Develop some "radar" about the room, what they're open to across the table; it changes room-to-room and even hour-to-hour in the same room. Also, figure out how to act for "tape."*
Jay Kane/Talentworks New York

Being an actor is an extraordinarily difficult job. You must be working on your craft and your person all the time, staying abreast of what's going on and keeping your instrument tuned.

✦ *The actor has to be clear about what he wants and what he says. If he says he doesn't want to go out of town, but then misses out on an important project because it was out of town and gets mad at his agent, the agent is going to say,"Well, you said you didn't want to go out of town." Once you put qualifiers on your career, you are not going to have as many auditions.*
Ellie Goldberg/Kerin-Goldberg Associates

✦ *Keep active. Even a lousy Scene class will help you put less pressure on auditions.*
Jay Kane/Talentworks New York

✦ *It's very important for actors to network. If they have occasion to meet someone, follow up, stay in touch. It's important to keep your name afloat. I encourage proactivity, classes, showcases, open calls, trying to rustle up your own work.*
Jim Wilhelm/DGRW

✦ *You have to do a lot of work on your own. You sit around in circles with actors and everyone is saying, "well my agent didn't get me in on..." Now that I'm sitting in this chair, I can see that even the agent's best efforts sometimes go unnoticed.*
You need the combination of the actors doing their work and trying to get themselves in. I tell actors, "If you know the musical director or the company manager, go to them. You may get in that way easier than I can get you in." Getting an agent is not the be all, end all of the way to get work.
Laurie Walton

✦ *Keep your acting wheel greased by doing readings. This is very valuable. Everyone does them. You get to know a group of people.*
Charles Kerin/Kerin-Goldberg Associates

✦ *Make sure that we have enough pictures and up-to-date resumes without our having to call. If you are a musical comedy performer, be willing to go to an open call if we have discussed this is what you should do. It's important to keep working whether it's in a class or a workshop or a group. Networking is important, but don't expect that every time your friend gets an appointment that you will too, and just because you call or drop in all the time, that we are necessarily going to think of you more. You don't want to become a pest. It is a business, in spite of how casual it is.*
Gary Krasny/The Krasny Office

Important Details

- Have a pen and paper in hand when you return your agent's call.
- Check in often.
- Return calls promptly.
- Make sure your agent never gets a busy signal; get call-waiting.
- Pay attention to the common sense details of keeping lines of communication open.
- Trust your agent and follow his advice from picture and resume to what kinds of roles to audition for.
- Provide your agent with ample supplies of pictures and resumes without being reminded.

Clients and would be clients all want your agent's attention. What would be the best way to get your attention under the circumstances?

✦ *If I have to take time from my day to talk to you to see how your day is going, then I'm not on the phone doing what I am supposed to be doing. If you hear of a project, make a two-minute call, "I heard about this, is there anything in it for me?" That's the way to be a good partner.*
Ellie Goldberg/Kerin-Goldberg Associates

✦ *Actors need to understand that until 11:00 or 11:15 in the mornings, agents need to organize for the day, set up what Breakdowns they have to do, solve all the problems and handle the calls that came in at the end of the day before. This is organizational time for agents.*

If the actor can just wait until 11:00 or 11:15 to call to find out about their next important piece of news, they would receive a more favorable response from the agent. Anytime after 11:15 and before 4:30 or 5:00.
Gary Krasny/The Krasny Office

Networking

I know that networking is a dirty word to many of you. You say, "oh, I'm not good at all that," or, "I don't want to get a job just because I know someone," or "I'm here for art, not for commercialism," or, some other elevated actor-jargon we all use from time to time to keep ourselves from testing our limits.

The most effective networking is done with your peers. You're not going to be able to pal around with Stephan Daldry or Joe Mantello. But you can pal around with the next Stephan Daldry and the next Joe Mantello by becoming involved with playwriting groups.

If you make it your business to attend theatre wherever it's happening, you will begin to notice who the writers and directors are who are starting their careers. Focus on those whose work appeals to you. Let them know you like their work. Give them your card and ask to be on their mailing list, take them to tea.

After you've seen their work a time or two, let them know that you are available if they need anything. Become involved in their projects. You will all develop together. It's hard to break into what seems like the charmed circle because people would rather work with people they already know and trust, particularly when a great deal of money is at stake. But you can see their point, wouldn't you rather work with friends and proven talent?

It is difficult behaving naturally around those who are higher on the food chain than you. But if you are well-read and cultivate an eye and ear for what's good, you'll soon contribute to the conversation and move up the food chain toward your goals, one rung at a time.

Don't You Really Want to Work?

I'm a pretty quick study and, with concentration, I have the ability to memorize audition material and not hold the script for something as brief as a commercial. When I was a beginning actor, however, I would always hold the pages because my background had taught me to be self-effacing. It seemed to me that putting the sides down was too pushy. It would make them think I really wanted the job.

On the day I decided to stop holding the script and take responsibility for the fact that I really did want the part, I began booking jobs.

I looked up self-effacing in the dictionary: it means self-obliterating. Don't do it. Sir Laurence Olivier used to ask anyone working on a project whether there was anything in it for him. If Sir Laurence could admit he wanted a job, am I going to pretend I don't?

After successfully freelancing for a long time, when I finally signed with an agent I thought my own agenting efforts were over. From the perspective of time and research I realize that because I was passive, didn't educate myself, and had abandoned all the job getting tasks I practiced before, I missed out on exploiting my success in a more meaningful way. I had this idea that you have a breakthrough and then everything just comes to you. Maybe for Julia Roberts, but even then, I doubt it. I just had no idea how the business works. It's a business, not a fairy tale. And it's a 24/7 business. That's the life you've chosen.

Some actors become angry when they have to tell their agents how to negotiate. They feel the agent is not doing his job if he has to be reminded to go for a particular kind of billing or per diem.

We all need encouragement and respond to reminders. I don't like to admit it, but I can almost always do better with prodding. I might not think so initially, but my extra efforts usually pay off.

If the agent does everything perfectly, great. But it's your career. It's up to you to know the union minimums and how to get your price up. It's up to you to figure out the billing you want and to help the agent get it. You are getting the 90%. Not only is it your responsibility, it's a way for you to be in control of your destiny in a business where it is too easy to feel tossed about by the whims of the gods.

Agents' Expectations

Before I talk about the agents' responsibilities, let's hear what agents expect from actors:

✦ *If I sign an actor for a year, I expect consistent callbacks. I expect, at least, growth. I'm not going to look at somebody's track record and say, "you've been out on fifty things here and you haven't booked a job; I don't think there's anything we can do here." It's difficult. It's very competitive. If I've believed in someone from the beginning, and if I see progress, if I see growth, and if I see the potential is still there, then I'm encouraged.*
Kenneth Kaplan/The Gersh Agency

✦ *I expect that they'll prepare the audition material ahead of time, they'll show up punctually, that they won't be afraid to go out on a limb and take some risks with the material, that they will return my phone calls promptly.*
Gary Epstein/Phoenix Artists

✦ *I expect my client to be on time, to be prepared, to be pleasant and to do the best job he can. Once I get you in the door, you are on your own. I think actors should not be afraid to take control of the situation. If they want to start over, they should say so.*

If they want to read different sides, they should ask for it. If they want to read another character, they should go for it. If they feel they were ignored, they should say so and not complain and whine to the agent.

The actor is a grown-up and casting directors are not demi-gods. They are people even though they have total control. I don't mean the actor has to complain, but he should make it known that he wasn't comfortable.

Gary Krasny/The Krasny Office

✦ *A client will say, "are you angry with me because I didn't do so and so?" No. I'm giving you choices and opportunities. You make the decision and I'll go along with it. If I think it's a self-destructive point, I'll tell you. We can talk about it, but it's ultimately your decision.*

Tim Angle/Manager/Shelter Entertainment/Los Angeles

The agent puts his reputation on the line by sending you in and you put your reputation on the line by the quality of your work.

What the Actor Has a Right to Expect

All we want an agent to do for us is get us meetings for projects we are right for. This seemingly simple request requires of agents all the things that actors need to do: be informed and be professional, network, stay visible, and communicate.

As we maintain our credibility by giving consistently good readings, the agent maintains his credibility by building trust with the buyers. When he calls and says, "see K Callan, you won't be sorry," the casting director knows he won't.

If K Callan gets the job, the agent must be ready to do a wonderful job of negotiation, one that will make the actor (and the agent) happy and, at the same time, make the casting director feel he got a bargain.

The agent has all our responsibilities and more. The agent must maintain relationships with all of his clients and with the buyer. He must keep the buyers happy so that he can have return business.

If your agent can't get you in, the buyer won't get a chance to see your talent. Once in the buyer's presence, it's up to you to make your agent and the casting director look good by your brilliant work.

What the Actor Doesn't Have a Right to Expect

The actor/agent relationship is no different than any other relationship. No one likes to be presumed upon.

Don't

- Call your agent at home unless it's an emergency.
- Drop by the office unannounced expecting the agent to be available to talk to you.
- Expect your agent to deal with your personal problems.
- Arrive late (or very early) for meetings.
- Distract the staff when they should be working.
- Bad-mouth the agent to others. If you have a problem, be a grownup - take it up with your agent.
- Interview new agents behind your agent's back.
- Call and say, "what's happening?"
- Expect the agent to do all the heavy lifting.

Although many agents will be amenable to your dropping by and visiting with the secretary, etc., it's best not to take these things for granted. After all, you want these people to be available to do business for you. If they are talking *to* you, they're not talking *about* you.

If you are not feeling confident about yourself, go to class, talk to a friend, a therapist, whatever, but don't burden your agent with that information. Will he feel like using up his credibility telling them that you are the best actor since Meryl Streep when he knows you can't even get out of bed?

If you are not up to auditioning well, tell your agent and postpone or cancel the audition. You are not only not going to be performing well enough to get the job, but people will also lose confidence in you and in your agent's instincts. It will be harder to get the buyer to see you next time.

Although the agent's main job is to get you appointments and negotiate, I believe you also have a right to expect him to consistently view your work and to consult with you before turning down offers. Your agent's advice regarding career moves is one of the things you are paying for. He is a conduit to and from the casting director; he should convey feedback honestly about the impression you are making.

Make it clear you are ready to hear the bad with the good, but you would prefer he express it in a constructive manner. Instead of "you did lousy," how about "you were late," "you were not prepared," or "the casting director said your energy was down." Let him know that you want to remedy any problems, but that you need to know what they are. It's hard to assess auditions accurately without feedback.

Most agents want to give advice about pictures and resumes, so do consult them. They may want you to send them your credits online so they can texture your resume and put it on their own letterhead. The picture is your agent's sales tool and he knows better that you what he needs, so make sure he gets what he needs to represent you best.

If I were writing a book I thought agents would read, I would suggest that periodically they call the actor in (whether the career is going well or not) and ask the actor to rate the agency. Is the actor feeling comfortable? Cared for? Serviced properly? An annual mutual rating wouldn't be a bad idea. Is the actor doing his part? Is feedback good? Pictures and/or resume need updating?

At contract renewal time perhaps the agent himself (instead of an assistant) would call and say: "K, how are you? It's contract renewal time, I'd love to have you stop by and have a cup of coffee with me (lunch?) and have us talk about our relationship. We're still happy, we hope you are, but I'd like to get some input from you on what kind of job we're doing. Come in. We'll talk. We'll celebrate your contract renewal."

If I were suddenly a hot commodity, it would sure be a lot harder for me to think about leaving for the attentions of WME because I had been made to feel valued by the agent even before my big break.

Staying In Touch

Keep in touch with your agent by being a good partner. Call with updates, a lead or to show him new pictures.

✦ *Give me a tool I can use. Actors need to do 50% and I will do the other 50%.*
Nancy Curtis/Harden Curtis Associates

Los Angeles manager Ric Beddingfield says actors should make it a point to be seen by their agents once a week. Although most agents agree grudgingly that actors and their agents need to be in constant contact, most also agree that they hate the phone call that says, "what's going on?" They translate that into "where's my appointment?"

It's like when you were little and your mom said, "what are you doing?" when she meant, "is your homework done?" If you think about it from that perspective, perhaps you'll find a way to have a conversation that does not make the agent feel defensive. If you are calling to say you've just gotten a good part in a showcase, or just began studying with a new teacher, or "hey, did you see the new play at The Public? It's great, don't miss it," the agent is going to be a lot happier to hear your voice or see your face.

When Laurie Walton was still an agent, she said:

+ *The only thing I'm not enjoying is that actors call me daily. It's tough. I would never be unkind because I've been there, but on the other hand, I think a lot of them are taking advantage and that's the part I'm not enjoying because actors can really be annoying.*

It's because everybody wants to work. I understand that hunger and need but it's interesting for me that they're not using their heads more and knowing that it's probably going to have the reverse effect.

A Los Angeles agent put it succinctly, "my worst day is when I talk to more clients than buyers."

Remember that while you are taking the negative step of whining to your agent, you are avoiding taking some kind of positive action for your career.

E-mail

If you really really want to make a bad impression on an agent and guarantee that he will never be interested in you, e-mail him little notes, flyers and reminders of your existence. It may save you money and time sending off these little message, but while you are doing that, you're clogging up his e-mail.

A non-obnoxious way to stay in touch presents itself when you drop off pictures and resumes. Call ahead and say that you are going to drop off new pictures and want to pop in. Once there, ask the receptionist if you can just stick your head in and say "hi." Late afternoon is best.

You can just be in the neighborhood and drop by to show a new wardrobe or haircut. Then be sure to do that; just poke your head in. Don't sit down unless asked and if asked stay no more than five minutes. Be adorable and leave.

If you are depressed and need to really talk, call ahead and see if your agent has time for you. Suggest a cup of coffee after work or, if he has time for a snack in the middle of the afternoon, you can bring goodies. Everyone is happy to see a treat in the late afternoon. Since most people bring in sweets, bring a basket of strawberries or blueberries. Agents will be happy to see something healthy.

Make the effort to speak to everyone in the office and call them by their names. Get to know your agents and their support staff on a person-to-person basis. Learn something about each one of them and take notes so you can establish personal relationships. You'll be able to say something that is not about you and/or the business. That will make all of you feel more comfortable.

♦ *We don't need phone-ins. We don't have the manpower. We encourage people to let us know when they are in showcases. Obviously, we can't go to all of them. We usually end up picking reliable ones. By that, I mean reliable by reputation of the theatre, quality of production, the kind of cast they usually attract, and also the material. We stay away from showcases that do a lot of the classics. I don't think they're going to show the actor in anything we could sell them for.*
Peter Strain/Peter Strain & Associates

It takes two energy-expending components to make any merger work. The agent must work hard for you all of the time and you need to deliver all of the time. If you don't stay abreast of what's in town, what shows are on television that might use your type, what you got paid for your last job, which casting directors you have met, who your fans are, and/or if you are late or ill-prepared for appointments, the agent is going to get cranky.

If he doesn't drop you, he'll stop working for you. Worse, you'll get work anyway and he won't feel able to drop you. He'll just hate you.

If you are diligent, do everything you can do for your own career, and consistently give your agent leads that he doesn't follow up on, then you're going to get cranky and leave. It takes two.

Wrap Up

Details

✓ officially notify the previous agent that you are leaving
✓ take pictures, resumes, tapes, quotes, billing, etc., to new agent's office
✓ meet everyone in the office
✓ make map of where everyone sits

The Actor's 90%

✓ stay professionally informed
✓ network
✓ follow through
✓ communicate
✓ make informed suggestions
✓ get in a good acting class
✓ have call-waiting/dependable voice mail
✓ check in and return calls promptly
✓ stay visible
✓ be loyal
✓ pick up the sides
✓ be punctual
✓ do great auditions
✓ give and get feedback

The Agents 10%

✓ arrange meetings with casting directors, producers and directors
✓ arrange auditions
✓ negotiate
✓ network
✓ maintain credibility
✓ communicate
✓ make informed decisions
✓ stay professionally informed
✓ return phone calls promptly
✓ guide career

⚞ 12 ⚟

Stand-Ups/Children

Whoopie Goldberg, Roseanne Barr, Chevy Chase, Jerry Seinfeld and Ray Romano are all examples of performers and stand-up comics who crossed over into films and television. Today, added to that list are performers who write, stage and act in their own one-person shows. Theatrical agents don't deal with this type of performer usually, so I interviewed a few agencies who specialize in this area of the business. The longer version of this information is in my book, *How to Sell Yourself as an Actor*, but here's the *CliffsNotes* version.

✦ *We've definitely steered toward a very personality oriented comic. A charismatic style comic. "The Tonight Show" might use a comic because they're a very good comic in terms of their writing: a structural comic who writes a perfect setup and a punch line. Some of those comics wouldn't crossover into a sitcom because they might just be joke tellers. We want somebody who is a very full bodied character a la Roseanne, Tim Allen, Seinfeld. The development and casting people are looking for that. They are already walking in with a character. Some comics have stronger skills in that area.*
Bruce Smith/Omnipop Management

In Franklyn Ajaye's terrific book of interviews with other comics, Jay Leno talked about his seven year rule.

✦ *"I've always told comedians that if you can do this for seven years, I mean physically make it to the stage for seven years, you'll always make a living. If you've been in the business longer than seven years and you're not successful, there's probably another reason. Sex, dope, alcohol, drugs - - you just couldn't physically get to the stage. Sam Kinison is sort of an example. He was funny, hilarious, but near the end he couldn't get to the stage anymore. No matter how popular you are, promoters are not going to rehire you if you miss gigs."*
Franklyn Ajaye, *Comic Insights*[14]

✦ *A lot of comedy clubs across the country have closed, but there are still some in the Northeast, so it's easier to keep a comic working there as they start to develop. The more stage time they have, the better they become. We encourage them to get into acting classes, not to become actors, but just to start. We want to know what their long range goals are. In order for a comic to become popular, he needs television exposure. If you can support that with a strong act, you're going to have a good career.*

Tom Ingegno/Omnipop Management

✦ *I wouldn't assume that just because you are a comedic actor that you can do stand-up. Soap opera people try to do stand-up. Most of them, because they are so pretty, have not lived that angst ridden life that comics have. It becomes a frivolous version of comedy. The first thing you want to establish with an actor that is going into comedy is: Do they have a natural feel for it? Do they have comedic rhythm for it? There are many actors who are wonderful with comedy, but can't do stand-up. You need the stage time.*

Bruce Smith/Omnipop Management

✦ *A comedic person has to have the backing of theatrical training, otherwise you're looking at a personality-oriented project. Many stand-ups came out of theatre and did stand-up as a means of survival.*

Steve Tellez/CAA

✦ *I would say to really know whether you have any place in the comedy business at all, that you would have to give yourself at least two years. Less than that is not enough. The first year you'll spend just trying to get your name around, trying to get people to know who you are so they will give you some stage time.*

It's a long trip. Just like an actor. Don't seek representation with five minutes of material. You need to keep working. The next thing to do is to try to get work in road clubs. It's very important to get the experience. There is limited experience if you just stay in one city.

Bruce Smith/Omnipop Management

The personal appearance agents that I spoke to supported what I learned from theatrical and literary agents: no one is interested in one-shot representation.

If you get a guest shot on *30 Rock* and call a credible agent with that as an entree, he will probably talk to you. But if you don't have a track record of credits (they don't all have to be as important as *30 Rock*) then the agent is not going to be interested. 10% of one episode isn't enough to get you on his list and share all his introductions and hard work.

If you have written a one-person show and Disney is interested, that might be interesting to a stand-up agent. However development deals go south with regularity and if you don't already have a stand-up career going for yourself, personal appearance agents are not going to be interested. They want people who have been playing clubs in and out of town and have the stage time and some good material.

Stand-up and performance artist shows are a bonafide way to be entrepreneurial about the business, but there are no short-cuts to theatrical/comedic maturity. You gotta do the time.

Children in the Business

I don't think life as a child actor is a good deal for kids. You only get one shot at being a child and being taken care of. If you blow that, you are up a creek.

The tabloids make a lot of money running stories on the messed-up lives of former child actors. Lindsay Lohan anyone? I know you think you and/or your children could never have those problems. Maybe you won't. But at least think seriously about the possibilities before you take the next steps. If your child is paying your rent, the balance of power tips and there is no more family hierarchy.

In the recent past, more and more television shows market to kids in the 8-12 age range on the Disney Channel, Nickelodeon, Cartoon Network and The Hub. This has led to a big demand for child and teenage actors.

The shows makes being famous look appealing, but never deal with the repercussions of all that attention, freedom and scrutiny.

✦　*Disney Channel spokeswoman Patti McTeague said the 24-hour media microscope can magnify existing issues for any actor, especially a teenager.*

"So much of what they say and do, especially in their private lives, is chronicled and transmitted to millions of people and the Internet adds a whole new twist," McTeague said. "Nobody, nobody can live under that spotlight for very long and not have it impact them in some way. Some deal with it differently than others."

Disney, like Nickelodeon, offers a "Talent 101" course that seeks to prepare young talent for the pressure that might lie ahead, such as being recognized while shopping and managing their image online. The Disney course includes a licensed clinical psychologist and addresses privacy concerns, taking care of oneself (physically and emotionally), coping strategies and security issues.

Dawn C. Chmielewski and Amy Kaufman, *Los Angeles Times* [15]

It's difficult for even adult actors to withstand the "no rules environment" that comes with stardom. Some are able to hold onto themselves and stay normal at first, but with so much adulation and attention, pretty soon they do what human beings are supposed to do, they adapt. And it can be ugly.

♦ *"Some of these young actors start to become caught up in the show-business machine," said John Kirby, an acting coach who has worked with young actors on such films as "The Chronicles of Narnia: The Lion, the Witch and the Wardrobe" and the 2003 "Peter Pan." "The visibility is so great that honestly, I'm not surprised that so many of them are having problems."*
Ibid.[16]

When I've cautioned parents in the past about putting the kids and teens in the business, they frequently say, "Oh, but she loves it. She's dying to do it. This is what the wants."

I'm sure she would like to eat ice cream all day too. Her brain is not fully developed yet and she doesn't have the capacity to make an informed decision. It's the job of parents to protect children from themselves. Years ago, a casting director wanted my then-10-year-old daughter to read for the lead in a movie. I believed then and I believe now that there is no way a ten-year-old plays a lead in the movie and is still a ten year old at the end of that process. The movie turned out to be an iconic movie. The young girl who played the lead pretty much had a train wreck of a life afterwards. Parents beware.

But If You Are Still Determined

Professional experience is not necessary, but it helps. Children's agents don't expect professional pictures. Kids change quickly, so it's a waste of money. Agents are perfectly happy to see snapshots. Mail them with a note giving vital statistics: age, weight, height, coloring and any activity that had your child in front of people and taking direction.

What your child absolutely must be is comfortable with people. Happy. Confident. Gregarious. If the picture interests the agent, he will ask to see the child. He will want to speak to the child alone.

Parents are invited out while the agent gets a feel for how the child handles the meeting that would be part of an audition, so make sure you're dealing with a reputable agent.

If you are a child reading this, know that agents are impressed when a child makes his or her own arrangements. It means he is motivated, organized and responsible. A children's agent told me that her role model for a child actor was a client who at thirteen who had done lots of local theatre, called SAG, got a list of agents and sent in pictures himself. He got the first job he went for: a tour of *The Sound of Music*.

Children are paid the same per day as adults and will be (all things being equal) expected to behave as one. No sulking, tantrums or crankiness. They don't like it when adult actors do that either!

Set-Sitters

Parents should be prepared to ferry children to auditions and if the child books a job, to be on the set at all times. Not only is it a SAG rule that a parent or designated set-sitter of some type be provided, but it is *never* wise to leave your child in an adult environment on his own.

Someone needs to be your child's advocate. No matter what the job or how good the management, the studio is in the business to make money. Someone must be on set who is not afraid of losing his job if he says that the set is too hot or the kid needs a break. We all want to please and do a good job, but certain rules must be followed.

You or your designated representative should be always with your child. You and your child should know the SAG-AFTRA and Equity rules about school time, rest breaks, overtime and wardrobe fittings.

You don't have to be a member to access the SAG-AFTRA website to check out the helpful information and videos available for kids and parents at *www.sag.org/content/for-kids*.

I'm pretty much not a fan of managers as I feel they charge an extra 15% for services that any good agent expects to provide, however, a manager can be helpful at the beginning of a child's career not only being a conduit to a good agent, but educating both parent and child about work permits, audition behavior and other details of the business.

While some agents don't mind helping with those things, some tell me they prefer managers so they don't have to spend that time. Talking with parents on sets, I realize that there is a "mother's grapevine" of sorts and mothers do a pretty good job of educating themselves and each other, so if you want to forgo the manager, the SAG-AFTRA content for kids mentioned above is a good place to start.

It's imperative that parents recognize their role in the process.

✦ *"What parents have to understand is, they are the excess baggage that comes along with the talent," says Innovative Artists' Claudia Black. "It's the parents' responsibility to make sure the child is prepared, on time and has rehearsed the scene.*

"....If agents can't get along with the parent, they won't take the kid. It's really not just about the kid being amazing," says Cunningham Escott Dipene's Alison Newman. "It's a joint thing, fifty-fifty."

Alexandra Lange, New York Magazine[17]

Parents may be viewed as excess baggage, but they are necessary baggage. If your child begins to work steadily, it's a full time job for one of the parents. It might be exciting at first, but when/if your child is really successful, you might find yourself not only in an inferior position on the set but, also with your child.

Examine your reasons for putting your child under such stress. If your child is motivated and has dreamed of acting forever, that's one thing. If he's just excited about seeing himself on television or if you always wanted to act, but didn't, you should step back and reconsider.

Wrap Up

Stand-ups

✓ need fifteen to twenty minutes of material to begin
✓ need a persona
✓ should have theatrical training
✓ gotta do the stage time

Children

✓ can get by with a snapshot to begin with
✓ are paid as an adult, must behave like one
✓ must be able to talk to anyone
✓ require a set-sitter
✓ are only half the package, it's the parents' job too

Parents

✓ get a full time job if the child starts working, but no respect
✓ should consider all the ramifications of their decision

⊰ 13 ⊱

Managers

Can a Manager Sell What an Agent Couldn't?

Many beginning actors seek a manager because they have been unable to attract an agent. If a credible agent doesn't feel he can sell you yet, why would a credible manager think he could?

If the agent didn't see anything marketable, is the manager going to create something? It could happen, but I'd want some proof that the manager has access and developmental skills. Some managers latch onto every new face in town, hoping that somehow one of them will hit.

Beverly Robin Green is an entertainment attorney in San Francisco. Although she works mainly in the music field, her words about managers are valid for managers of actors:

◆   *Artists often say they would like to put together a professional "team" of a manager, agent, and attorney. They ask me where they can find the manager or agent. That is a good goal and a good question. It opens up a lot of other questions about what the artist is really looking for, and what the artist has to offer. The different roles that managers and agents play in the music business are difficult to define. They even vary widely in their own categories and from situation to situation, and this can be confusing. Also, what an artist wants may simply not be available to them at this point in their career, especially with respect to managers and agents, who usually work strictly on a commission basis. Another problem is that many of these people simply do not want to bother working for an artist until the artist has already gotten a record contract or is otherwise already taking off in their career. This creates a "Catch 22" situation for the aspiring artist.*

On a practical level, in selecting a manager, you need to define what you need the manager for and see if that role fits the person you are considering. A lot of times people say they want a manager to get them gigs (wrong, but often done) or to get them a record deal (in California anyway), but a manager who is unknown and inexperienced is not going to have the knowledge, connections or reputation to be of much help in this regard.

Beverly Robin Green, *OnStage Magazine*[18]

I spoke to an agent who had been asked by a friend to review a contract between the friend's daughter and a manager. Not only was the manager taking 15% of any acting work, but 15% of *any* work, even the actress' day job. Huh? When the agent asked the actor for the rationale, he was told, "well, when I'm working the day job, I won't be available for work." Does that make any sense to anyone?

Many feel that handing off their careers to a manager increases their cachet in the business. It may. It may not.

Hampered by outdated agreements with the performers unions and what they deem unfair/unregulated competition from managers, some excellent agents are choosing to dump their agency franchises and become managers themselves, but that's mostly in Los Angeles.

These people have credibility as far as I am concerned, but I wonder about all those people who just woke up one day and decided to call themselves managers.

A manager that is connected and in love with you could surely enhance your career. If you just graduated from one of the Leagues and scored well in their showcases, many agents and managers may be giving you their cards. Don't let anyone rush you into signing anything. Check out all possibilities before you decide.

It's possible that a manager could get to you before you meet any agents and say, "hey, don't bother meeting any agents, I'll take care of that for you when you are my client."

I see where they are coming from on that. If you are going to have a manager, one of the services you might expect would be his input into your agent selection. However, if you never even meet any agents, how will you make an informed decision regarding the need for a manager?

It makes sense for you to meet with anyone who calls you just to see what they have to say. You'll see how others see you and your career, and with every meeting you'll become more confident.

Don't be in a hurry. These people are all salesmen and make brilliant impressions. You'll be tempted to sign in the moment, but you're not just magically going to pick the right person; you'll need to do some research. The right manager, one who is connected and passionate about your career, can definitely make a difference. But so could the right agent.

When Julia Roberts came to New York (already connected because of brother, Eric Roberts), her manager, Bob McGowan, uncovered a part for her in the movie *Satisfaction*. The part called for a musician, so McGowan enrolled Roberts in a crash drum course and enticed William

Morris into repping her for the job.

So, if we had McGowan for a manager and happened to have the looks and charisma of Julia Roberts, who knows what could happen?

Ultimately, Roberts dropped McGowan and opted for William Morris, and no manager, choosing to not have any more layers between herself and her employers.

Managers Can't Legally Procure Work

Although the law has rarely been enforced, managers are not legally allowed to procure work. That's the business of those people who have licenses from the state: you know, the agents.

✦ *Actress Jennifer Lopez has filed a petition with the California Labor Commissioner accusing her former manager of violating the state's Talent Agency Act by procuring employment on her behalf.*

The primary charge centers on whether Benny Medina was acting as her agent. Because Medina allegedly procured and negotiated work for her, the petition is requesting that all oral and engagement contracts she had with Handprint be voided. Those contracts saw her pay 10% of earnings from movies and television, 15% of her music, recording and publishing earnings, and 10% of her earnings from ancillary activities, including fashion and cosmetic interests.

Chris Gardner and Peter Kiefer, Hollywood Reporter[19]

Actress Nia Vardalos won a similar lawsuit against her ex- manager:

✦ *The state court judge has refused to hear a challenge from Nia Vardalos' ex-manager to California's law barring managers from acting as talent agents. Tuesday's ruling by Los Angeles Superior Court Judith Chirlin sets the stage for the state labor commission to go ahead with a proceeding next week against Marathon Entertainment for performing as an unlicensed talent agent for Vardalos.*

The management company sued Vardalos in January for failing to pay 15% commission from her earnings from the hit comedy feature, "My Big Fat Greek Wedding," which she wrote and starred in.

Dave McNary, Daily Variety[20]

No one believes that Lopez and Vardalos have suddenly found religion and don't want to be in business with someone who is breaking the law. The lawsuits look like a way to avoid paying commissions and get out of a contract. The fact remains that it's illegal for a manager to procure work for you.

The Association of Talent Agents webpage has this to say:

✦ *The job of the ATA agent is to create opportunities, procure and negotiate employment for clients, and counsel them in the development of their careers. Agents in most states must be licensed by the state, city or appropriate governing body. Managers are not regulated nor are they required to have a license. Under law, managers may not procure employment for artists or negotiate without a licensed agent, and any person who renders Agent services without a license may have their contract invalidated and be forced to relinquish any commissions paid.*
www.agentassociation.com/frontdoor/faq.cfm

And if he's not going to procure work for you, why would you be wanting a manager? There are other reasons, believe it or not.

When It Makes Sense to have a Manager

- Managers are a definite plus for child actors who need guidance and whose families have no show business background. A manager usually places the child with an agent, helps select pictures and wardrobe, monitors appointments, and some even accompany the child to meetings and auditions.

- If you are entering the business and need someone to help you with pictures, resumes, image, etc., managers can be helpful. However, many agents delight in starting new talent and consider this part of their service.

- When you are at a conglomerate agency and it's too intimidating and time consuming to keep in touch with twenty agents, it might be advantageous to have a connected manager in your corner.

- Changing agents is easier when you have a manager because the manager does all the research, calling, and rejecting of the former agent.

If agent-changing is the only reason you have engaged the services of a manager, it's an expensive antidote to one uncomfortable meeting. If you have the credits to support getting a good agent, you can do that on your own. If you don't, the manager can't create them.

I have a few friends who feel the presence of a manager enhanced their careers, at least momentarily. One in particular said her agents were considering dropping her, so she and the manager made her more attractive to the agents by getting some jobs themselves. They read the Breakdown and the actress delivered her own submissions to the casting offices.

If the manager got a call for an appointment, the actress went in. If she got the job, they called the agent to make the deal. The agent became more enthusiastic about the actress for a while, but ultimately dropped her. The agent's earlier disinterest signaled what he had already decided: that the actress was no longer appropriate for his list. In that case, the manager, though helpful, only delayed the inevitable.

And his actions were, of course, illegal.

What Do Managers Think Their Job Is?

From The National Conference Of Personal Managers website:

♦ *First, let's state what a personal manager is not. A personal manager is not an agent (whose role is to obtain employment). A personal manager is not a publicist (whose role is to generate publicity). Nor is a personal manager an attorney (whose role is to provide legal counsel). And, a personal manager is not a business manager (whose role is to provide accounting, investment, and other financial services).*

A personal manager advises and counsels talent and personalities in the entertainment industry.

Personal managers have the expertise to find and develop new talent and create opportunities for those artists which they represent. Personal managers act as liaison between their clients and both the public and the theatrical agents, publicists, attorneys, business managers, and other entertainment industry professionals which provide services to the personal manager's clients.

Even though the NCOPM says managers "have the expertise...", there is no governing body that certifies this to be true. You could decide right now to be a manager, hang a shingle, announce your new business to the trades, and wait for the 8x10s to flood your mailbox. So just as you would in any business situation, ask questions. It's difficult to withstand a full court press from someone who professes to love you and want to help you, but find out if this person has the credentials to do that. See more at *www.ncopm.com*.

✦ *There are managers out there who wine and dine actors after the showcases and tell them not to meet with agents themselves and not to return their phone calls, particularly mid-level agents. Those actors might really be missing out. They should be meeting with the agents and making their own decisions. It's possible they don't even need a manager.*
Gary Krasny/The Krasny Office, Inc.

A highly visible friend of mine recently lost a job because her manager discouraged her from speaking to her agent. The actress lost the job over money that would make no difference in her lifestyle. The agent might have prevailed in the negotiation.

The job was in a show that is now a huge hit and would have given real momentum to my friend's career. I kept saying, "why don't you call your agent and ask what is happening?" Her reply? "I don't want to make my manager mad."

On those two unsuccessful occasions when I did have a manager, the thing I liked least was that I was not supposed to talk to my agent myself. If I can't talk to my agent, how can he have a clear understanding of who I am and what I can do? The more you hand off your power to another, the less control you have over your destiny.

Researching Managers

Check out managers the same way you do agents. First, Google them to see if there is anything online. Then ask friends if they have heard of anyone who has a manager who has enhanced their careers.

If you know any casting directors well enough to ask, ask them if there are managers they work with that they could recommend.

If you do set up a meeting, be prepared to ask how the manager got into the business, what casting directors he has relationships with, and who is on his client list. I've heard that managers really don't like their other clients to know about each other.

Too bad for them, *www.imdpro.com* not only lists managers, legal team and publicists, but you can cross reference to see the list of clients for all those teams.

Go in with your own idea of how long you are willing to be committed contractually and how much you are willing to pay in commissions. Just because he asks for 15% doesn't mean you have to pay that. These things are negotiable.

Don't be short-sighted. Have faith in yourself. Whether you are choosing an agent or a manager, don't just take the first person who shows some interest. Even though they may not seem that valuable to you at the moment, you have assets to protect: your face and your career.

You may say, "well, so what if someone wants to charge me 25%. Right now, I am making nothing. If I make money, I'll just give this person 25%."

That's fine today while you aren't making any money. But when you do work, you'll have a manager taking 25%, an agent taking 10% and Uncle Sam taking up to 50% leaving you with only 15% from all your work.

Wrap Up

Managers

✓ can provide guidance
✓ take a larger percentage than agents
✓ can't legally procure work
✓ are not governed by industry standard contracts
✓ are not licensed by the state
✓ Google them or check with *www.imdbpro.com*
✓ check with casting directors
✓ check other clients
✓ ask informed questions
✓ negotiate length of contract and commissions

◁ 14 ▷

Divorce

It's hard to decide where to place information a~ that don't work out. When I first started writing about agents, ⌐ ~ the book talking about this painful subject. Vigilant folk pointed out that you have to have an agent before you can leave them. True, but some people who are reading this book already have an agent and are contemplating leaving. They need guidance.

Don't skip this part just because you don't have an agent yet. You may learn some valuable lessons that will help you avoid a divorce in the future.

If an actor is not working, frequently he thinks it's the agent's fault and the actor fires him. But the agent might not be the problem.

Valid Reasons for Leaving

If your agent won't return your calls, if he's been dishonest, or is not getting you out, those are legitimate reasons for leaving. Maybe you and your agent have different ideas regarding your potential. This is something that should have been ironed out before the contract was signed. When that conversation comes later in the relationship, reality must be faced. Sometimes careers change and actors feel they can be better serviced by agents with a different set of contacts.

Perhaps your level of achievement in the business has risen. Through brilliance, or possibly a lucky break, you have now become an actor of greater stature than your agent. This is very possible if fortune has just smiled on you.

Actor/agent relationships are just like any other relationship: as long as it's mutually rewarding, it thrives. When it's not, things must change.

Actors and agents seek each other for mutual gain. The agent must see money-making potential to be interested in taking on partial responsibility for your career. While thirty-five perfectly credible agents may pass on you, number thirty-six might fall in love, send you to the right place with the right material and the right director, and suddenly

...rse, it can happen the other way too. One minute you're hot ...next moment you're not. You didn't necessarily do anything so ...ently to get un-hot; frequently getting hot works the same way.

Jumping ship every six months (which a lot of actors do) only serves to hurt the actor because everybody knows about it and it shows that the actor can't necessarily get a job because something's wrong and it's not because of the agent.
Gary Krasny/The Krasny Office

Before you replace and/or bad-mouth your agent, consider the following possibility:

Maybe It's You

- You might have gained or lost weight and now no one knows what to do with you.

- You may be traveling into a new age category and have not yet finished the journey.

- You might be getting stale and need to study.

- You might be having personal problems that are reflected in your work; after all it's the life energy that fuels our talent and craft.

- The business might have changed, beautiful people may be in (or out).

How many projects can you list that had parts for you for which you were not seen? And were there really parts for you? Your physicality and temperament must not only match the parts, but also you must have the credits to support being seen for significant parts.

What part would you have been sent up for on a Broadway show? Yes, it would have been nice if you had played the part in that film, instead of Brad Pitt, but no agent would have sent you up for the part. You're not yet far enough along in your growth or visibility.

Maybe the reason you want to change agents is that your friend seems to be getting more auditions than you. It is hard to listen to others speak of their good fortune when you are home contemplating suicide, but before you get out the razor blade:

Consider

- Although you may frequently be seen for the same roles as your friend, there are aspects of your persona that are not the same.

- It cuts both ways. There have surely been roles that you were right for and your friend was not. You and your friend may be on different career levels.

- Perhaps your friend has not been totally candid in the descriptions of his auditions.

- It just might not be your turn right now. Be patient, it will be.

Maybe it's time for you to be proactive: get into a class, court casting directors, do a showcase and mount your own project.

Measure your progress against your own development. Judge your relationship with your agent on whether or not it is mutually rewarding and respectful. If your agent has been dishonest with you or if there have been financial improprieties, those are valid reasons to leave.

Is Your Agent Doing His Part?

How can you tell if it's just not your turn, or if the agent isn't tending to your business? You can check with casting director friends, writers, directors, and anyone else you know in the business. If you are being as involved as you should be, you'll be abreast of current projects so that you will have a realistic idea concerning projects for someone like you. You can't be a hermit and expect to work.

Ask your agent what you can do to help get more auditions. Discuss casting directors you would like to meet. Have a list of two or three who cast material for which you are appropriate in both career and type.

Check with friends you trust to see if they have had any activity. Let them know you are not fishing for information, but just checking on your own paranoia. "Is my agent just not sending me out right now or is nothing going on?"

Drop by your agent's office with new pictures. Is the phone ringing? Are they calling other clients? Or is the place calm with inactivity? If the office isn't busy, this may give you and your agent a chance to chat.

Communication

If you and your agent can't talk, that is a serious problem.

✦ *The biggest problem in the actor/agent relationship is lack of communication.*
Martin Gage/The Gage Group

✦ *Most of the time, when someone leaves, it's mutual. The bottom line is that it is the actor's career. If he is not happy, then it's up to him to say, "can I have a meeting because it's been too long?" And then we will say, "what have you seen that you weren't up for? Or what have you heard of?"*

He might mention a project that he wasn't in on and we'll pull it out and see that on that project they were looking for stars or younger or whatever. As soon as we talk about it, the problem is usually over. It's important, though, to have the conversation.
Ellie Goldberg/Kerin-Goldberg Associates

✦ *If the agent screws up a job, I think you should leave. If you don't get any appointments and you think you should be getting appointments, then you should move on to someone who is excited. If the agent doesn't take your phone calls, that's really a sign that there is something wrong. Sometimes you just have to get a fresh outlook. It works both ways.*
Gary Krasny/The Krasny Office

If you are not getting auditions you might be unhappy enough to leave your agent, but be realistic. If there are no parts in your category right now, a new agent can't change that. He might send you out on auditions you're not right for and make you feel busy, but you're still not going to get a job you are not right for.

Not everyone gets to do everything. Agents tell me the number one reason that a working actor leaves one prestigious, credible agent for another is that the actor sees his career in a different venue. If he's on soaps, he wants to be on primetime. If he's a television star, he wants to do films. When an actor becomes a star in one area of the business, that some people, seeking to curry favor, tell the actor how terrific he is and how he can do anything. That may not be true.

Research your peers. Have they made that change? Some people have enormous breaks come their way, but not everybody is going to make a movie and not every actor is going to do Broadway.

✦ *I think you know what you've been submitted for, how many appointments you've gotten. You have to take the explanation of the agent and weigh it.*
Jeff Hunter/William Morris Endeavor

Every agent has different contacts. An agent may have great theater contacts and no film contacts, but tells the actor he does. If you were that actor and the agent didn't get you a film audition for a year, you'd be getting the sense that he wasn't being truthful.

✦ *We have to tell actors what we think they can realistically expect. That pierces their dreams sometimes and they move on.*
Jeff Hunter/William Morris Endeavor

The larger agencies are not in the business to handle less profitable jobs. They either drop you, or their lack of interest will finally tell you that you're no longer on their level. This is the moment when you might be sorry you left that swell agent who worked so hard to engineer the big break for you.

Will he want to see you now? He might. He might not. It depends on how you handled it when you left.

Sometimes the manager suggests the actor leave an agent. That can be a good idea, but it's also possible the manager is jealous of the actor/agent relationship and is seeking to put himself in a more powerful position.

Maybe you want to leave because the magic has gone out of your marriage, just as the magic can go out of a traditional marriage if both partners don't invest energy. Check the discussion of the actor's responsibilities in chapter eleven for ideas on how to add energy to your relationship.

Agents Divorce Actors Too

It's worth noting that agents divorce actors too. Sometimes it's for bad behavior (*life's too short*) or lack of communication, sometimes it's because the agent's list has gotten too big/costly and he needs to trim, but most times it's because an actor is not working, although some agents don't let even that shake them,

✦ *When a client of mine doesn't get work, I just figure the people who are doing the hiring are morons. I know when I take on a client that it's for life. I have so much faith in my own taste that I would never lose faith in a client.*
Phil Adelman/The Gage Group

If you are both willing to save the alliance, that will take a lot less energy and resourcefulness than going through the "just learning to get to know each other" period involved in any new relationship.

The bottom line is you're not getting work. Beverly Anderson said:

✦ *"It doesn't make any difference what the reason is. If you're not getting work, you have the right to leave and if you're smart, you will leave."*
Beverly Anderson

Don't Wait Until It's Too Late

Just like anything else, if something is bothering you, speak up. Candor comes easily to very few people. Most actors have a need to be liked and it's not pleasant to confront people.

If you are not going out, call your agent and try to have a face to face meeting. He knows as well as you that you are not going out. Tell him you are concerned; I'm sure he is too. Don't make him defensive. Let him know you understand that this is a mutual problem.

Ask him if there is anything you can do. Ask if he has heard any negative feedback. Whatever you do, don't just start interviewing for a new agent and bad-mouthing your present agent to your friends.

It's easier to whine to bystanders about your dissatisfaction than to confront your agent, but that's childish, ineffective, dishonest and makes you look bad. If you intend to succeed in this business, you'll have to do better than that.

✦ *Early on, at some moment, discuss problems with the agent. There are actors who hide in their kitchens, angry because they have not had auditions. By the time they can't stand it any longer, they call and tell you they're leaving. We're not omniscient; we don't know sometimes what is happening or not happening.*

We have meetings every week at the office and discuss all the clients and we might know someone is dissatisfied. But even if we miss it, you are obliged to come in and speak to your agent, not an assistant, because you are signed by the agent. Then we'll discuss it. We'll have a discussion and try to solve it.

Fifi Oscard

Leaving Your Agent

If you waited too long and it's too late for a talk, or if the talk didn't help, at least leave with a little class. Though it might be uncomfortable, get on with it.

✦ *I would be very upset if someone with whom I've had a long relationship fired me by letter. I think it would be the ultimate rudeness, ingratitude, lack of appreciation for the work I've done. Get past the guilt, the embarrassment. I'm owed a certain consideration. Deal with it. I understand the difficulty, but that's not an excuse.*

Phil Adelman/The Gage Group

So be a grown-up. Your agent deserves the courtesy of a personal meeting. Go in and talk to him. Explain that, for whatever reason, it's just not working. No need for long recriminations. No excuses. Not, "my wife thinks," or, "my manager thinks." Simply say, "I've decided that I am going to make a change. I appreciate all the work you have done for me. I will miss seeing you, but it just seems like the time to make a change. I hope we'll see each other again."

Write your own script. No need to be phony. If you don't appreciate what the guy has done and don't think he's done any work, just skip it.

Talk about the fact that you think the relationship is no longer mutually rewarding. Leave your disappointment and anger at home. Be straightforward and honest and you'll both be left with some dignity. You may see this person again, and with some distance between you, you might even remember why you signed with him in the first place. Don't close doors.

If you are leaving because your fortunes have risen, the meeting will be even more difficult because the agent will be upset to see you and your money leave. Also, your newfound success has probably come from his efforts as well as yours. But if you are really hot and feel only WMA, CAA, or some other star agency can handle you, then leave you must.

Tell him you wish it were another way, but the vicissitudes of the business indicate that, at a certain career level, the conglomerates have more information, clout, and other stars to bargain with, and you want to go for it.

If you handle it well and if he is smart, he will leave the door open. It has happened to him before and it will happen to him again. That doesn't make it hurt less, but this is business. He will probably just shake his head and tell his friends you have gone crazy, "this isn't the same Mary I always knew. Success has gone to her head."

He has to find some way to handle the rejection, just as you would if he were firing you. It will not be easy to begin a new business relationship, but you are hot right now and the world is rosy.

Wrap Up

Questionable Reasons for Leaving

✓ no recent work
✓ manager pressure
✓ agent disinterest

Better Remedies than Leaving Agent

✓ improve communications with your agent
✓ take a class, study with a coach
✓ do a showcase
✓ court casting directors
✓ put your own project together

Clear-Cut Reasons for Leaving

✓ lack of respect
✓ dishonesty

- ✓ communication didn't help
- ✓ differing goals
- ✓ personality differences
- ✓ sudden career change for better or worse

Speak to Agent

- ✓ before things get bad
- ✓ before interviewing new agents

✒ 15 ✒

Researching the Agents

There are various categories of agents and managers: big, small, credible, wannabes, beginning, aggressive, just getting by. Since rep/client relationships are personal, any classifications I make are subjective. I'm presenting the facts as best I can, based upon my research and personal experience both in interviewing these agents and my years in the business. You must digest the information and make your own decisions.

There are new agents building their lists who, like you, will be the stars of tomorrow. You could become a star with the right one-agent office and you could die on the vine at CAA.

There are no guarantees, no matter whom you choose. The most important office in town might sign you even without your union card if your DVD and/or resume excites them. But mostly they don't take developmental clients. They want you when you are further along. Whomever you choose, if you are to have a career of longevity, you can never surrender your own vigilance in the process of your career.

Evaluate Carefully

If you read carefully, you'll make a wise decision using client lists, the agents' own words, and the listing of each agency. Don't write anyone off. In this business no one knows anything. I love my agent, but you might hate him.

There are nice people who are good agents and there are nice people who are not. There are people who are not nice who are good agents and so on. Just because I may think some agent is a jerk doesn't mean he is. And if he is, that might make him a good agent. Who knows?

If you read all the listings, you will have an overview. I've endeavored to present the facts, plus whatever might have struck me about the agent: this one was once known as "The Goat Lady", that one was an Equity rep.

Some agents have survived for years without ever really representing their clients. They wait for the phone to ring. Some agents talk a better game than they play. I believe it would be better to have no agent than one who is going to lie to you.

Agent Stereotypes

We all know the stereotypes about agents: they lie, that's their job. While some agents lie, most don't. Most are hard-working, professional, regular people who, like you, want to make it in show business.

Like you, they want to be respected for their work, go to the Academy Awards and get great tables at restaurants. And again, like you, they are willing to put up with the toughest, most heartbreaking business in the world because they are mavericks who love the adventure and can't think of a single thing that interests them more.

Many who read this book are just starting out and will be scanning the listings for people who seem to be building their lists. Many of those agents have great potential. Some don't.

Who's Included in This Book?

Anybody who would talk to me? Only those agents that I could actually in good conscience, recommend? It seems inappropriate for me to try to play God about who is worthy and who is not.

On the other hand, I don't want my readers to think I would recommend everyone who is in the book. That automatically makes anyone not in the book suspect.

When the first edition of this book was published, I only included agencies, other than the conglomerates, whose offices I personally visited and interviewed. Today, in the interests of time and geography, there are a now some that I have only met on the phone and my updates have been done on the phone. The majority of the profiles are still based on personal interviews.

Most of the time I went to the office because that was most convenient for the agent. Seeing the office also helped refine my thinking about the agency. I didn't meet everyone in every agency, or all the partners, but I did always meet with a partner or an agent who was acting as a spokesman for the company. I could be wrong in my judgments, but at least they are not based on hearsay.

It's a good bet that if an agent is not included in the book then I didn't know about them or had no access to information about them.

Number of Clients

The number of clients listed at the end of an agency profile only refers to theatrical clients, unless otherwise specified. Just as the box office receipts reported in *Variety* might be inflated for business reasons, an agency may under report the size of their list. In reality they may have more clients than they can reasonably represent and they would just as soon not publicize that fact.

The general agent-to-client ratio to look for is at least one agent for every twenty to twenty-five clients. Although a good agent will tell you that's the number to shoot for, it's rare that you get an agency that adheres to that, regardless of the numbers they report.

Realistically, how is an agent going to give personal attention to more than twenty-five clients? And also realistically, unless the clients are on series, how is a small agent to pay his bills with only twenty-five clients?

Most of the profiles in this book list a few clients from the agency's list, but some of the agents would not release any names lest they leave someone out. In those cases they frequently give me a list and invite me to choose names. Sometimes I've gleaned names from trade ads paid for by the agency. Some information comes from trade columns devoted to information on artists and their reps. Some comes from *www.imdbpro.com*.

About Imdbpro.com

As mentioned earlier in the book, *www.imdbpro.com* has a wealth of useful information if you know where to look. I know a lot of it isn't accurate because when I researched agents, I saw the site listed many who I know have been out of business for a while. Even so, enough data is correct that you can draw reasonable conclusions for your purposes.

For instance, I saw that my agent, The Gage Group is ranked 189. Imdbpro doesn't list 189 out of how many, but as you look further you can at least see who is above or below that. Leading Artists, which has a perfectly fine list of clients is listed 742 and Abrams Artists is 33.

Is this based on their number of clients? Of how many clients have worked recently? I wrote to Imdbpro and their answer was pretty vague, seemingly based on numbers of inquiries and might change daily.

I asked specifically because I was totally confused as to how they rated CAA, ICM Partners, WME and UTA, thought by most of us to be numbers 1-4 on any given day. CAA was #4, while UTA, a hugely successful agency was #14. WME was #5 and ICM Partners was (for heavens sake!) listed as #13. No matter which agency I looked up, I never could figure out who was #1.

In the meantime I checked on my own rating which was 13,264 on that particular day. I found that if you click on the rating, you can find a little chart that shows what your rating was on a particular day. I noticed that on December 17, 2006 my rating was 6,927 while a week later it was 10,315. In April 2007 I was 11,256 one week and the very next week I was 3,917. There was a notation that I had been on two shows the first week and I guess the bump came the next week. I looked up various agents and their histories and saw how much they fluctuated from week to week, so for myself anyway, I think the lower number is more useful for ego gratification than an indication of my career. I suspect the numbers are just as squishy for the agents.

There are several tabs at imdbpro: clients, staff, main page, etc. Size of client list is mentioned randomly, mostly for the largest agencies and bears scrutiny under the clients tab. You'll be able to discern whether the client is an actor, writer, host, musician, commercial actor, etc., relative to the agent listed beside the name.

While *www.imdb.com* is free, *www.imdbpro.com* charges for access. At first, I thought I would only subscribe briefly, but now I consider my subscription a necessity.

You can get a free two week trial to evaluate the service.

Less Is More

Once you feel you actually have something to interest an agent; a reel, a play in production, and/or some swell reviews from decent venues, be discriminating in your quest for representation.

Don't blanket the town with letters. Target three agents that seem right for you and ration your money, time, and energy. It's more likely to pay off than the scattershot approach.

Agents are already inundated with DVDs and reviews and while they are all looking for the next hot actor, there are only so many hours in a day. Don't waste their time or yours.

If you are just starting, don't set your heart on CAA, choose someone who is at your level so you can grow together.

A job is not an automatic entree. As you have probably noted throughout this book, most agents are not interested in a one shot deal.

Don't despair. Agents agree that new blood is what keeps the industry going. Even if you have thirty pairs of shoes and swear you will never buy another, if you see shoes that captivate you, you will buy them. The trick is to be captivating, or more importantly, marketable.

Body of Work

In my experience researching agents for actors, writers, and directors, I keep learning that agents are interested in a body of work. They want to see a progression of you and your product. They want to know that they are not squandering their hard won contacts on someone who doesn't have the ability to go the distance. They won't be able to buy a cottage in the south of France on their commissions from one job. Neither will you.

Like attracts like. You will ultimately get just what you want in an agent. I believe you can get a terrific agent if you become a terrific client. There are no shortcuts. And today is not the last day of your life.

In her book, *My Lives*, Roseanne quotes a line from Sun Tzu's *The Art of War*, which she says everyone in Hollywood has read. It basically says: "The one who cares most, wins."

Kevin Bacon/Referrals

As you read the agency listings, you will see that many of the agents, though they will look at query letters, are not open to being contacted by new people who have no one to recommend them.

If you don't know anyone, remember "The Kevin Bacon Game" It's the same concept as the play/movie *Six Degrees of Separation*, which contends that anyone in the world can find an association with anyone else in the world through six associations: in "The Kevin Bacon Game" it only takes three degrees, and in some cases, less.

It goes like this. Your mother shops at the same grocery store as Kevin Bacon, or in my own case, I have worked with Kyra Sedgewick who is married to Kevin Bacon. Ostensibly, if I had a script I wanted to get to Kevin, I ought to be able to get it to him through Kyra.

If you track all the odds and ends of your life, you should be able to produce somebody who knows somebody who knows somebody who can make an authentic (however tenuous) connection to someone who can make a call for you. Otherwise you are just querying/calling cold.

If you can't come up with a connection, write the best darn letter in the world and knock some agent on his butt. However, if you can score at "The Kevin Bacon Game," it would be best.

Remember

✓ Your first agent is you. You must be your own agent until you attract someone who will care and has more access than you. It's better to keep on being your own agent than to have an agent without access or passion.

✓ Make yourself read all the listings before you make a decision.

✓ Mass mailings are a waste of money. There is no use sending WME or CAA a letter without entry. It's pointless to query someone you have never heard of. If you have no information about the agent, how do you know you want him? Take the long view. Look for an agent you would want to be with for years. Be selective.

✓ Don't blow your chances of being taken seriously by pursuing an agent before you are ready.

✓ Although rules were made to be broken, presuming on an agent's time by showing up at his office without an appointment or calling to speak to the agent as though you are an old friend, will ultimately backfire. Observe good manners and be sensitive to other people's space and time.

✓ Getting the right agent is not the answer to all your prayers, but it's a start!

✓ Call the agency and confirm the address before you send anything. Things change quickly. The agency won't know it's you.

16

Agency Listings

⊿ About Artists Agency ⊾

1650 Broadway, #1406
at 51ˢᵗ Street
New York, NY 10019
212-581-1857

Renee Glicker majored in both art and theatre at the State University of New York. Told that if you could be happy doing anything other acting, you should, she tried audience development in Florida and realized that she had to act. Returning to New York, she scored a national tour of *They're Playing Our Song* followed by commercials, cabaret, television, films and off-Broadway.

Her day job at night as a waitress at The Comic Strip, allowed her to observe the developing careers of Adam Sandler, Wanda Sykes, Jerry Seinfield, Chris Rock and others. She absorbed so much of their process that up-and-coming comics asked her to critique their work. Club booker Lucien Hold (who became her mentor) noticed and asked Renee to help open a management company for comics.

When Renee heard that a big theatrical agency wanted to create a comedy department, she arrived with her clients and began booking immediately. Three years later, she opened her own agency. Celebrating her 13th anniversary in 2011, Renee reflected on her track record. She booked more actors on *The Sopranos* than any other agent in New York and has actors working as much in film and on television as in theatre.

Clients include Robert Prescott (*Michael Clayton*), Emilio Del Gado (*Sesame Street*), Phyre Hawkins (*Book of Mormon*), Trisha Jeffrey (*Sister Act*), Kevin Duda (*Book of Mormon*), Richard Crawford (*WarHorse*), Mike Backes (*Jersey Boys*), Christina Calph (*Tower Heist*), Johnnie Mae (*Boardwalk Empire*) and Allison Semmes (*Book of Mormon*).

Agents
Renee Glicker
Client List
150 plus freelance

≤ About Face Talent Agency ≥

419 Park Avenue South, # 607
New York, NY 10016
212- 221-1518

Jenevieve Brewer came aboard The Carson/Kolker Agency in 2003 to run their commercial, hosting and print divisions, but her reach soon exceeded that goal and she began expanding into legit. She was so successful that in late 2010 owner Barry Kolker decided to create a separate agency called AboutFace, to nourish Jenevieve's expanding list of working actors.

Jenevieve is joined by Alice Skiba and Sonia Stewart in repping their list of clients that work in film (*Cop Out, One For the Money, Too Big to Fail, Smurfs, Premium Rush, Fugly, True Grit*) and on television (*Law & Order SVU, Blue Bloods, The Onion, The Onion Sports Network, Delocated, Body of Proof, Boardwalk Empire, You Don't Know Jack, Rubicon, Are We There Yet, Bored to Death, Mercy and White Collar*). They only book principal roles. Check *www.imdbpro.com* and *www.aboutfacetalent.com* for more information.

Agents
Jenevieve Brewer, Alice Skiba and Sonia Stewart
Client List
50

⚒ Abrams Artists Agency ⚒

275 7th Avenue
btwn 25th & 26th Streets
New York, NY 10001
646-486-4600

Through resourcefulness, determination and an eye for talented agents and artists, Harry Abrams has headed or partnered a string of agencies over the years starting in the 60s with the commercial powerhouse Abrams-Rubaloff and evolving into the powerful and respected theatrical and literary office that is the Abrams Artists Agency of today.

Abrams runs the motion picture and television departments in Los Angeles and leaves the New York office in the hands of vice-president and managing director Robert Attermann.

Neal Altman, Rachel Altman, Beth Blickers, Danielle Delawder, Genine Esposito, Ellen Gilbert, Tracey Goldblum, Amy Mazur, Kate Navin, Paul Reisman, Bonnie Shumofsky, Maura Teitelbaum, Amy Wagner and Tracy Weiss join Atterman shepherding their distinguished list of clients. Mark Turner reps hosting talent.

Their theatrical list includes Roma Downey (*Touched by an Angel*), Judith Ivey (*A Bird of the Air*), Ron Leibman (*The Sopranos*), Otto Sanchez (*Curb Your Enthusiasm*), Kathy Searle (*My Man is a Loser*) and others. AAA also handles children and young adults. Clients come to this agency through referral.

Agents
Robert Attermann, Neal Altman, Rachel Altman, Beth Blickers, Danielle Delawder, Sarah Douglas, Genine Esposito, Ellen Gilbert, Tracey Goldblum, Ron Gwiazda, Morgan Jenness, Amy Mazur, Kate Navin, Paul Reisman, Bonnie Shumofsky, Maura Teitelbaum, Joe Thompson, Amy Wagner, Billy Serow, Tracy Weiss and Mark Turner

Client List
2073

◢ APA ◣

Agency for the Performing Arts
250 W 57th Street #1701
near the corner of 8th Avenue
New York City, NY 10019
212-657-0092

Founded in the 1960s by expatriates of MCA/ICM, APA is known as a hot breeding ground for comics and hot music and concert performers. APA's muscle doesn't stop there, however as they also rep theatrical, literary, hosting, commercial and voiceover talent.

Headed by APA president and CEO James H. Gosnell, the agency has offices in Beverly Hills, New York and Nashville.

In October 2010, Nikki Finke's *Deadline Hollywood*, quoted talent department head and new partner, Ryan Martin who said that "APA had doubled its revenues in the past five years." Since they rep Gary Oldman, Lewis Black, Craig Ferguson, Betty White, Louis CK, The Kardashians and a host of others at the top of their careers, that isn't hard to believe.

Martin began his career in 1996 at UTA and spent time at Writers & Artists before joining APA in 2002. He oversees 14 agents and 250 actor clients. The lion's share of agents service clients from the Beverly Hills office, but Mark Berkowitz, Barry McPherson and Megan Brown all operate out of the New York.

APA reps actors, musicians, comedians, authors, scriptwriters, composers, hosts, directors, music producers, teens and young adults.

Unless you're checking out comedy clients, APA's website, *www.apa-agency.com*, is pretty useless. Much more info at *www.imdbpro.com*.

Agents
Mark Berkowitz, Barry McPherson and Megan Brown
Client List
1028

ᴁ Andreadis Talent Agency, Inc. ᴂ

119 W 57th Street, #711
E of 7th Avenue
New York, NY 10019
212-315-0303

With a father in vaudeville, it's no surprise that Barbara Andreadis joined the family business and became an actress. Like many of us, she left the business when she had children. Her kids are grown now but instead of returning to her acting career, Barbara opted to continue mothering a different group, her family of actors who, of course will always need her. Barbara trained at The Bonni Kidd Agency, ultimately running that agency for two years before starting her own business in 1983.

Andreadis says she "carries no generic types, only individuals." Her clients include Steve Greenstein (*Confessions of a Shopaholic*), John Solo (*Man on a Ledge*), Jill Nicklaus (*Chicago, Movin' Out, Cats*), Karen Lynn Gorney (*Saturday Night Fever, All My Children*), Beau Baxter (*Too Big to Fail*), Amanda Gabbard (*Christmas in New York*), Dan Grimaldi (*The Sopranos*), Roberta Wallach (*The Sopranos*), Catherine Wolf (*Wall Street 2*), Jason Furlani (*Man on a Ledge*), Leif Riddell (*Rescue Me*), Tony Devito (*New Amsterdam*), Mark Manley (*The Boy from Oz*), Evangelia Kingsley (*Coram Boy*), Rosalind Brown (*Footloose*), Catherine Fries Vaughn (*Beauty & the Beast*), Marilyn Sokol (*Old Jews Telling Stories*), Richard D'Allesandro (*Forrest Gump)* and Peter Ratray (*The Country Girl*).

Barbara is one of the first agents casting directors call for musical talent and with many Actor's Studio members on her list, she also has an eye for dramatic actors. She also handles children and young adults.

Agents
Barbara Andreadis
Client List
75

◅ Ann Wright Representatives ▻

165 W 46th Street, 10th Floor
just E of Broadway, in the Equity Building
New York, NY 10036
212-764-6770

When Ann Wright came to New York after training as an actress at prestigious Boston University, she joined the casting pool at CBS. Like many other actors who have an opportunity to explore other areas of the business, she realized there were other ways to use her creative skills and became the assistant to legendary William Morris agent, Milton Goldman.

Ann cast commercials at an advertising agency and then worked for both Charles Tranum and Bret Adams before opening her own commercial talent agency in 1964.

Still thought of first as a voiceover and commercial talent agency, the legit department continues to thrive with clients working in theatre, film and television.

Daughter Susan was a trade show producer before she ran Ann's west coast office for eight years. Now she has returned to New York where she has created a successful youth division for both legit and commercials.

AWR's theatrical list includes Gino Conforte (*Angels & Demons*), Laksh Singh (*Pendejo*), Kimberly Amato (*Party Girls*), Isobel Rose Costello (*Hallows' Eve*), and Rick Toscano (*Somewhere Tonight*).

Agents
Ann Wright and Susan Wright
Client List
20

◣ Ann Steele Agency ◢

330 W 42nd Street, 18th floor
btwn 8th & 9th, W of Port Authority
New York, NY 10036
212-629-9112

Houston native Ann Steele taught at Kansas State Teachers College and at a community college in Illinois, was a Girl Scout Executive in Georgia and the Director of the Girl Scouts for the Borough of Queens before showbiz entered her brain via her son's involvement in a program called Acting by Children.

When Ann started raising money for the group, she observed managers checking out kids, picking choice clients and recognized a ripe business opportunity. She and a partner started their own business representing young actors like Jason Alexander, Michael E. Knight, Kevin Kilner, Alex Winter, and Christopher Steele.

Ann retired from managing in 1989, reemerging as an agent in 1997. Her list includes Orville Mendoza *(Peter and the Starcatcher, Pacific Overtures, Roadshow, Miss Saigon, Adrift in Macao)*, Julius Thomas III *(Gershwin's Porgy and Bess, Scottsboro Boys, Xanadu)*, Anne Otto *(Hugh Jackman: Back on Broadway)*, Antyon Le Monte *(The Book of Mormon)*, Bill Bateman *(Gypsy, Hello, Dolly)*, John Salvatore *(Jersey Boys, Las Vegas)*, Michael Biren *(Billy Elliot)*, Carole Denise Jones *(Mamma Mia!, Whistle Down the Wind)*, Gene Jones *(No Country for Old Men)*, Josh Sassanella *(Rock of Ages, Mamma Mia!)*, Leonard Sullivan *(Hairspray, A Chorus Line, High School Musical)* and George Riddle *(Onion News Network)*.

While I was there, a client called and said she was in the neighborhood and would Ann like a nice iced coffee? How can you not love a client like that? And how can you not love an agent who is known in some circles as Ragtime Ann?

Agent
Ann Steele
Client List
120

⚓ Archer King, Ltd. ⚓

1650 Broadway # 407
on 51ˢᵗ Street, btwn 7ᵗʰ & Bdway
New York, NY 10019
212-765-3103

Archer King has been a showbiz fixture since he produced *Two Blind Mice* on Broadway with Melvyn Douglas in 1949. At one time or another, I think Archer has either worked with or discovered everyone in the business. He's 93 and still going.

He left producing to agent with the legendary Louis Shurr Agency, repping Bob Hope and the big musical stars of the day. Archer opened his own agency in 1957 and still has files on Jason Robards, James Dean, James Coburn, Martin Sheen, and the three-year-old Ronny Howard, all actors he helped at the beginning of their careers.

From 1963-67, Archer imported and distributed such foreign films as Roman Polanski's *Knife in the Water* and Volker Schöndorff's *The Tin Drum*, as well as films from Ingmar Bergman.

While head of theatre for RKO Television, he was responsible for the television productions of *The Gin Game* starring Hume Cronyn and Jessica Tandy, and *Sweeney Todd* starring Angela Lansbury (for which Archer won a Golden Ace Award).

Although some guides list Archer repping actors, comedians, composers, directors, legitimate theatre, lyricists, packaging, producers, screenwriters, and musical theatre, Archer says his main business these days is developing and packaging movies.

Clients include Sophia Robbins (*Sunday Serenade*), David Barraso (*Saving Melanie*) and Levi Wilson (*The Invisible Life of Thomas Lynch*). Archer has a perceptive eye for talent, and is known to give newcomers a helping hand. Read more about Archer at *www.archerkingltd.com*.

Agent
Archer King
Client List
Freelance

⚐ The Artists Group ⚐

1650 Broadway, #1105
at 51ˢᵗ Street
New York, NY 10019
212-586-1452

Originally an actor, Robert Malcolm never intended to be an agent, but in 1984 when his agent, Peggy Grant offered him a job with time off for auditions whenever he needed it, he agreed to work for her. Peggy died a few months later and left the agency to Robert and he has not been to an audition since.

In 1986, Robert had changed the name of the agency to PGA and in 1990 to The Artists Group. In 1991, when Robert bought the Los Angeles based agency also named The Artists Group, his NY office became The Artists Group East.

At that time, Robert became bicoastal and left his New York office in the hands of Cynthia Katz.

In 2007 he closed his LA office and moved back to New York and he reclaimed his old name, The Artists Group.

He compacted his client list and now mostly reps an impressive list of longtime clients including Loretta Switt, Nancy Dussault, Tony Lo Bianco, Judy Kaye, Mickey Rooney, Jamie Farr, Amanda Plummer, Bonnie Franklin, Theodore Bikel, Carole Cook and Tammy Grimes.

Though committed to his longtime family of actors, Robert is always looking for hot new talent and continues to look at all pictures and resumes.

In 2009, Cynthia Katz left to start Gotham Talent.

Agents
Robert Malcolm
Client List
65

⚔ Atlas Talent ⚖

15 E 32ⁿᵈ Street, 6ᵗʰ fl.
just E of 5ᵗʰ Avenue
New York, NY 10016
212-730-4500

In 2000 Lisa Marber-Rich, Jonn Wasser, John Hossenlopp, and Ian Lesser left Don Buchwald & Associates to create a broadcast agency providing talent for on camera and voiceover commercials as well as for promotionals, narrations, trailers, books on tape and animation.

In 2010, they celebrated the beginning of their second decade by opening a Los Angeles office.

Lisa was an Account Manager in advertising at Bates, DMB&B, and Foote Cone Belding, Ian Lesser was in film production at Tribeca Studio, and Jonn Wasser was in marketing at Radio City and worked as a freelance entertainment writer with articles published in Details and other national magazines.

Marilyn McAleer was head of Creative Services at HBO, Lifetime and National Geographic before joining Atlas to head Promos. Heather Vergo, Meredith McKeon, and Noah Suchoff comprise her team in repping talent for promos, trailers and documentaries.

Using Integrated Switch Digital Network (SDN), whereby the voice can live in Los Angeles and work in New York via the telephone, has resulted in Atlas' impressive international list that includes Ellen Burstyn, Stephen Collins, and Kathy Bates as well as their list of anonymous celebrity voices that reside all over the world.

For more information about this agency, check out their website at *www.atlastalent.com.*

Agents
Michael Guy, Lisa Marber-Rich, Tim Walsh, Jonn Wasser, Ian Lesser, Carli Fitzgerald, John Hossenlopp, Meredith McKeon and Noah Suchoff
Client List
120 VO and on camera

☜ Bauman, Redanty & Shaul ☞

1650 Broadway, #1410
at 51ˢᵗ Street
New York, NY 10019
212-757-0098

Richard Bauman and Wally Hiller created this agency in 1975. They are gone now and BRS is now the baby of David Shaul and Mark Redanty who joined as colleagues and are now the sole owners. Mark runs the show in New York while David shepherds the Los Angeles clients.

Mark Redanty studied acting/directing at Ithaca College and got a job working as a trainee at Raglyn-Shamsky Agency right out of college. He became an agent while at R-S and then worked for Richard Astor before joining (then) Bauman-Hiller in 1984.

Mark has been running the New York office since 1987, treating the business and clients with the care for which the agency is famous. This comfortable, easy style is reflected in Mark's approach to life and to the business.

He and colleagues Charles Bodner (Peter Strain) and Timothy Marshall (who trained at RBA) preside over a list of prestigious clients.

Some from their list include Robert Morse (*Mad Men, Tru*), Billy Magnussen (*Damsels in Distress*), Stephanie J Block (*9-5, Anything Goes*), Will Swensen (*Hair, Priscilla, Queen of the Desert*), Matt Lauria (*The Chicago Code*), Scott Wise (*A Chorus Line, Chicago*), Dennis Christopher (*Breaking Away*) and Michael Nouri (*Damages, Victor/Victoria*).

BRS only works with signed clients.

Agents
Mark Redanty, Charles Bodner and Timothy Marshall
Client List
80

⚞ bloc ⚟

630 Ninth Avenue, # 702
btwn 44th and 45th Streets
New York, NY 10036
212-924-6200

Canadian brother and sister Laney and Brendan Filuks moved to Los Angeles with no thought of ever being in the agency business: Laney left home to dance and act; Brendan to work for SONY. But as Laney became the go-to person whenever her agent, Dorothy Day Otis, needed help with the dance clients, she and Brendan hit upon the idea to open an agency with a focus solely on dancers. After all, their mother had her own dance studio, so they knew about dancers.

They chose the name because bloc means people coming together for a common goal. This agency reps actors, singers, choreographers and extreme athletes for legit, film, television, and print. Even though their New York office opened in 2001 shortly after 9/11, bloc NY managed to thrive.

Fatima Wilson, Jim Daly, Maegan Mishico and Emily Watson collectively run the New York office servicing clients ages 18 and up for film, legit, television and commercials.

Clients from their list include Daniel Solo, Shakira Marshall, Oneika Phillips, Justin Prescott, Ryan Rankine, Cristin Hubbard, Sandy Alvarez and Rebecca Kritzer. You can find out everything about the agency and who just booked what at their website *www.blocnyc.com.*

Agents
Fatima Wilson, Jim Daly, Maegan Mishico and Emily Watson
Client List
150

◢ Bret Adams ◣

448 W 44th Street
btwn 9th & 10th Avenues
New York, NY 10036
212-765-5630

The late Bret Adams created this agency and ran it with partner Bruce Ostler until January 2003 when Bret retired and Bruce Ostler and colleagues Margi Roundtree and Ken Melamed purchased the agency. Northwestern grad Bruce co-founded the Chicago improv group *Practical Theatre* and then moved it to NY for a successful run. After selling tv rights, he began a career creating, pitching, producing and writing for theatre, television and films.

Though he enjoyed the stimulation and access, the uncertain life of a freelance producer took a toll. In 1989-90, after a particularly long dry spell, Bruce's wife pointed out that by pitching projects and creating jobs for his friends, he had been honing skills for years. She suggested he take a new career path.

Bruce wasn't convinced, but in 1989 he began interning/assisting Bret Adams learning the business. He generally hated the whole thing until joining The Fifi Oscard Agency, the first place where he was able to put projects together. At that point Bruce began to really love his new career. In 1996, after five years at Fifi's, Bret called to offer his old assistant a partnership and a chance to create a new literary department.

Actor clients include Don Stephenson (*The Producers*), Carly Jibson (*Hairspray*), Ron Holgate (*Urinetown*), Matthew Cowles (*Ed*), Lindsay Crouse (*Flash Forward*) and Charles Keating (*Brideshead Revisited*).

In an effort to further clients' careers, their website, a co-venture with their clients, features their pictures, resumes and links. BA also has a respected literary department handling writers, directors, designers, and composers. *www.bretadamsltd.net.*

Agents
Bruce Ostler, Margi Roundtree, Ken Melamed and Michael Golden
Client List
About 100

CAA

Creative Artists Agency
162 5th Avenue, 6th Floor
btwn 21st and 22nd Streets
New York, NY 10010
212-277-9000

Gone are the days when CAA was the most powerful and largest talent agency. Forged by five William Morris refugees in 1975, CAA is still powerful and based on imdbpro's client numbers, the largest, but it's difficult these days to tell if CAA is clearly #1 anymore. Though the William Morris Endeavor merger certainly blended the upstart with the iconic, viewing CAA's formidable list of Oscar, Tony, Emmy and Grammy winners and just plain wonderful actors makes me wonder who could possibly be left for anyone else.

The New York office opened in 2003 when theatre heavyweight George Lane was lured from William Morris. Imdbpro says Lane now resides in Los Angeles leaving Mackenzie Condon, Jason Fox, Simon Green, Peter Hess, Cara Lewis, Joe Machota, Brian Manning, Diane McGunigle, Stephanie Paciullo, Eric Watenberg, and David Zedeck working the New York offices. With today's technology, geography may no longer be relevant.

Clients include Ryan Reynolds, Jennifer Anniston, Christina Applegate, Simon Cowell, Daniel Craig, Sean Pitt, Jeremy Piven, Brad Pitt, Nick Jonas, Faith Hill, Bill Maher, Alec Baldwin, Kevin Spacey, Stephen Spielberg, Meryl Streep and many, many more.

Since CAA is tight lipped about clients and agents, my intel is based totally on the trades and *www.imdbpro.com*

Agents
Mackenzie Condon, Jason Fox, Simon Green, Peter Hess, Cara Lewis, Joe Machota, Brian Manning, Diane McGunigle, Stephanie Paciullo, Eric Watenberg and David Zedeck

Client List
3167

✒ Carry Company ✒

20 W 20th Street, 2th floor
The Empire State Building
just W of 5th Avenue
New York, NY 10011
212-768-2793

Sharon Carry was working at a sports bar in 1990 when she got the idea to send out her well known patrons on the commercial auditions she read about in the trades.

She grew that business to include actors and athletes across the board, and now has clients working in film, television and on Broadway.

Carry has so many clients working in Los Angeles that in 2005, she opened a west coast office. She divides her time between the coasts and says she has a terrific assistant in each office.

Sharon concentrates on her signed clients, but also works on a freelance basis. She has a pool of about fifty kids and fifty adults. Don't postcard this agency unless you have something real to say. "Hello, how are you?" doesn't count. They prefer flyers when you are doing something. Sharon says she takes flyers and work very seriously.

For more information on Carry, check out her webpage at *www.carrycompany.com* and of course, *www.imdbpro.com*.

Agents
Sharon Carry
Client List
100

✑ Carson-Adler Agency, Inc. ✑

250 W 57ᵗʰ Street #2030
at Broadway
New York, NY 10107
212-307-1882

As a showbiz mom, Nancy Carson viewed a side of the business that inspired her to start an agency where children would be protected. She trained with children's agency Jan J. before joining with the late Marion Adler to form C-A in 1982. Daughter Bonnie Deroski finally grew tired of rejection and is Nancy's colleague along with Shirley Faison. Her background in management at the National Black Theatre and as another showbiz mom makes Shirley another perfect advocate.

Their roster includes Rachel Hilson (*The Good Wife*), Julianna Rose Mauriello *(Lazy Town)*, Andrew Keenan-Bolger, Andy Richardson, Jess LeProtto (all in *Newsies*), MacKenzie Mauzy, Matthew Gumley, Emma Rayne Lyle, Eric Nelsen, Cruz Santiago, Remy Zaken, David DeVries, Ben Liebert, Kiril Kulish, Frankie Galasso & Nathan Scherich (*Jersey Boys*), Imani Smith (*Lion King*), Eden Duncan-Smith, Zach Rand, Andy Jones, Eamon Foley, Madeline Taylor, Ken Barnett (*February House*), Luke Mannikus, Issadora Tulalian, Lara Teeter, Tyler Merna, Kara Oates (*Mary Poppins, 30 Rock*), Anthony Festa and Sam Poon.

Nancy's keen eye for kids with talent spotted Britney Spears, Ben Affleck, Matt Damon, Lea Michele, Donald Faison, Cynthia Nixon and repped them all when they were still under 18.

For parents seeking to learn the ins and outs of the business, Nancy's new book *Raising a Star* will answer all your questions. For submission policies, check their website *www.carsonadler.com*.

Agents
Nancy Carson, Bonnie Deroski and Shirley Faison
Client List
60

⊲ Carson/Kolker Organization ⊳

419 Park Avenue South #606
btwn 28ᵗʰ & 29ᵗʰ Streets
New York, NY 10016
212-221-1517

Created in 1992 by Steve Carson and wife Maria Burton-Carson, C/K was known as The Carson Organization, but in 2004 when Carson retired and sold the agency to colleague Barry Kolker (Henderson Hogan, Fifi Oscard), the name morphed into Carson/Kolker quietly reflecting both history and the present.

This agency's family approach provides nurturing as well as opportunity and is a good choice for actors of all ages looking for a home. Although casting directors think of them as one of the first places to go for infants, twins and children, C/K welcomes all age groups.

Clients include Kristen Alderson (*Starr Manning, One Life to Live*), Desiree Casado (*Sesame Street*), Ilene Kristen (*One Life to Live*), Eddie Alderson (*One Life to Live, Reservation Road*), Alex Charak (*As The World Turns*), Gerard Canonico (*Spring Awakening, American Idiot*), Georgi James (*Billy Elliot*), Heather Tepe (*Gypsy, Billy Elliot*) and Brynn Williams. C/K has clients recurring on *Boardwalk Empire* and *Louie* and many on tours of *Mary Poppins, Wicked, Shrek* and *A Little Night Music*.

Barry says he looks at all pictures and resumes seriously and that he has found clients from the mail. The legit department does not freelance, while the print and commercial department will freelance with the intent of signing.

Though they have similar names, Carson/Kolker is no relation to Carson-Adler.

Agents
Barry Kolker and Huascar Vizcaino
Client List
150 signed clients

✍ Carlton, Goddard and Freer Talent, Inc. ✍

1515 Broadway, #1132
New York, NY 10036
212-520-1023

Joel Carlton, Michael Goddard and Christopher Freer were all originally successful performers. Though they never worked together as actors, as agents they bonded as respected competitors and colleagues with shared goals and style. That kind of synergy produced Carlton, Goddard and Freer Talent, Inc. in January 2012.

Although Michael Goddard was a successful actor, his marketing background from Arizona State University couldn't be tamed and he spent a lot of time getting jobs for his actor friends. After checking Broadway, National Tours and Regional Theatre off his to-do list, his marketing skills won out and in 2006, he finished his last showbiz job one day and started work at Nicolosi & Co. the next.

Long Island native, Christopher Freer traded in his dancing shoes to become an agent for DDO and KSA in Los Angeles in 2000. Three years later, he headed to New York to create and head the New York office of Clear Talent where he stayed for the next eight years.

Joel Carlton's BFA from Webster University not only prepared him for 14 years as an actor, but served him well as a casting director and as an Equity business rep before he began his agenting career with The Luedtke Agency. He spent four years with DGRW and two at Jeanne Nicolosi before joining with Christopher and Michael.

Clients include Noah Racey *(Curtains, Never Gonna Dance)*, Hunter Ryan Herdlicka *(A Little Night Music)*, Megan McGinnis *(Les Miserables, Little Women, Beauty and the Beast)*, Dominic Colon *(John Sayles, Go for Sisters)*, T.J. Kenneally *(Blood Ties, Boardwalk Empire)*, Emily Tremaine *(Hallmark Hall of Fame's Firelight)*, Stephanie Umoh *(Ragtime)*, Will Blum *(Book of Mormon)* and Noah Racey *(Curtains, Never Gonna Dance)*.

Agents
Joel Carlton, Michael Goddard and Christopher Freer
Client List
90

✒ Clear Talent Group ✒

325 West 38th St., Suite 1203
between 8th & 9th Avenues
New York, NY 10018
212- 840-4100

Dancer/choreographer Tim O'Brien worked with Francis Ford Coppola, Stephen Spielberg, Michael Kidd, Pat Birch and Kenny Ortega before he hung up his dancing shoes and became one of the first representatives specifically for dancers working for both LA Talent and Kazarian/Spencer and Associates.

During that time, he also worked as a consultant for The Screen Actors Guild where he was instrumental in establishing a SAG dance category gaining huge protections that didn't exist before his efforts.

Tim created Clear Talent Group in 2003. New York CTG director Jamie Harris joined Clear that year and now heads the NY office. His list of dance credits ranges from Radio City Music Hall to Broadway to the Silver Screen. Paula Poeta moved from Brazil to Los Angeles for a BA in Theatre Arts at Long Beach State University that resulted in jobs at NBC, FOX, and MTV.

When she moved to New York, her background helped her book clients on *Law & Order: SVU, Blue Bloods, Louie, Boardwalk Empire, One Life to Live, Nurse Jackie, Good Wife and Gossip Girl, PAN AM, Person of Interest, Royal Pains, White Collar* and in numerous feature films.

Clients from Clear's list include: Jack Harding and Courtney Galiano (*Glee*), Chauna Bloom (*American Horror Story*), Brooklyn McLinn (*Rules of Engagement*), Rico Rodriguez (*Modern Family*), Logan Browning (*Meet the Browns*), Erica Mansfield (*How to Succeed in Business without Really Trying*) and Ayo Jackson (*Spiderman: Turn off the Dark*).

Check out their webpage at *www.cleartalentgroup.com*.

Agents
Jamie Harris and Paula Poeta
Client List
500-1000

⚓ Cornerstone Talent Agency ⚓

37 W 20th Street, #1108
just W of 6th Avenue
New York, NY 10011
212-807-8344

Though he was planning to use his 1991 history degree from the University of Wisconsin to become a lawyer, Steve Stone started training to be a general manager at Niko Associates the minute he graduated. He did that in tandem with being concessions manager eight shows a week at Tony Randall's National Actor's Theatre. In 1993 he was hired as assistant to Bob Duva (The Gersh Agency, Duva-Flack). When Duva left, he took Steve along as an assistant. A year later Steve was franchised as an agent. He created Cornerstone in September 1997.

Mark Schlegel (APA, Ambrosio/Mortimer, J. Michael Bloom, APA) planned to be a banker but when he landed a gofer job for Mitch Leigh working on *The King and I* as part of his communications major at Indiana's DePauw University, banking didn't stand a chance. His background somewhat mirrors Steve's since both began working for producers and also worked with/for Robbie Lantz.

Steve and Mark's list includes Sara Ramirez (*Spamalot, Grey's Anatomy*), Daniel Sunjata (*Dark Knight Rises*), Jon Michael Hill (*Eastbound & Down*), Anna Belknap (*CSI: New York*), Jefferson Mays (*The Best Man*), Bryce Pinkham (*Ghost - the Musical*), Tom Pelphrey (*End of the Rainbow*), Carole Shelley (*Billy Elliot*), Lois Smith (*True Blood*), Lillias White (*Fela*), Terrence Mann (*Addams Family*), Dominic Chianese (*Damages*), Jayne Atkinson (*Gossip Girl*), Isiah Whitlock, Jr. (*The Wire*), Gretchen Egolf (*Journeyman*), Edward Hibbert (*Curtains*), David Garrison (*Married with Children*), Katie Rose Clarke (*Wicked*), Ana Reeder (*Damages*), Joel de la Fuente (*Law & Order: SVU*), Darren Goldstein (*Damages*) and Damian Young (*Californication*).

Agents
Steve Stone, Mark Schlegel and Shannon Kelly
Client List
75

≫ DDO Artists Agency ≪

224 West 4th Street, #200
at W 10th Street
New York, NY 10014
212-379-6314

DDO's roots go back to 1969 in Los Angeles when Dorothy Day Otis created a top children's agency representing the kids from many hit shows including both *The Brady Bunch* and *Different Strokes*. Today DDO is a full service agency repping artists in every medium with offices in New York, Las Vegas, Nashville and Miami.

Bill Bohl and Abby Girvin worked for DDO in Los Angeles for years before purchasing the agency in 1995. Marlene Sutton (Sutton Barth Vennari) became their partner in 1996. At that point Bill created one of the first dance departments in LA, while Marlene joined with Maria Walker to build their successful commercial department.

Dance powerhouse Thomas Scott (Clear Talent) heads the New York dance and legit division. Armed with his degree in musical theatre from the Cincinnati Conservatory of Music, Thomas moved from Chicago to perform at the Paper Mill Playhouse in 1992. He then toured, did regional theatre and performed at City Center before choreographing and dancing on cruise ships. Tired of living out of a suitcase, he moved back to New York and cast for a while before becoming an agent. Thomas has made DDO the go to place for professional commercial and theatre dancers in New York.

Clients include Hettie Wright (*Oklahoma*), Kit Treece (*A Chorus Line*), Bryon St. Cyr (*Hair*) and Rhea Patterson (*Wicked, Guys and Dolls*).

DDO maintains offices in New York, Los Angeles, Las Vegas and Nashville. This agency opens all mail and is constantly looking to fill in gaps. Visit *www.ddoagency.com* for more information.

Agents
Thomas Scott
Client List
many many

⚓ DGRW ⚓

Douglas, Gorman, Rothacker & Wilhelm, Inc.

1501 Broadway, #703
btwn 43rd & 44th Streets
New York, NY 10036
212-382-2000

Barry Douglas, Fred Gorman, Flo Rothacker and Jim Wilhelm, created DGRW in 1988. Jim Wilhelm is now the sole remaining partner. An actor at fifteen, he was a stage manager, a PR director, a general manager and a casting director before becoming franchised in 1981. Jim is joined by three diverse colleagues.

Psychology major, Josh Pultz arrived from upstate New York in 1998 and began interning at DGRW within a week of graduation. Thinking he wanted to be a general manager, he left to work with producer Cameron Macintosh and general manager Alan Wasser but he missed DGRW and returned to become a franchised agent.

An actress when she interned at DGRW in 2005, Nicole Wichinsky now uses her Communications/Film Business and Theatre and degrees from the University of Miami repping clients.

DGRW's newest agent, Chad Pisetsky (Bauman, Redanty and Shaul) earned a degree in directing from the University of Michigan.

Names from the hundred or so actors on DGRW's list include Daniel Dae Kim (*Lost*), Kathleen Chalfant (*Wit*), Elaine Page (*Cats, Evita*), Cybill Shepherd (*The L Word*), Alice Ripley (*Next to Normal*), Patrick Page (*Spiderman*), Montego Glover (*Memphis*), Paige O'Hara (*Les Misérables*), Lynn Cohen (*Munich*), Harry Groener *(Crazy for You)*, Ron Raines *(The Guiding Light)*, Alan Campbell and others.

DGRW also represents directors, fight directors, choreographers, and musical directors. In addition to agenting, Jim teaches master classes at the University of Cincinnati/College Conservatory of Music.

Agents
Jim Wilhelm, Josh Pultz, Nicole Wichinsky and Chad Pisetsky
Client List
200

Don Buchwald & Associates

10 E 44th Street
just E of 5th Avenue
New York, NY 10017
212-867-1070

Former actor and producer Don Buchwald (Monty Silver, Abrams-Rubaloff) created the agency in 1977. DBA covers the spectrum of entertainment representation with divisions for film, theater, television, broadcast, commercial, literary, packaging, syndication, personal appearances and youth.

Although DB&A has many visible clients (John Shea, Piper Laurie, Kathleen Turner, Blythe Danner, Dick Cavett, Ian Bedford, Philip Bosco, Shanon Doherty), by far the most lucrative is Howard Stern who reupped his Sirius contract in December 2010 for five years for five hundred million dollars.

DBA executive VP Ricki Olshan oversees this vast agency. David Lewis, Jonathan Mason, Joanne Nici, Ricki Olshan, Rachel Sheedy and Allan Willig rep adult theatrical clients while Victoria Kress and Pam Goldman lead the Youth Department.

The DBA webpage news link lists newly cast clients and credits. Some from that page are: Bruce Altman (*The American*), Chaske Spencer (*The Twilight Saga: New Moon*), Dominic Nolfi (*The Jersey Boys*), Finn Wittrock (*The Illusion*), Zach Villa (*War Horse*), Cat Walleck (*War Horse*), Renee Felice Smith (*NCIS: Los Angeles*), Peter Riegert (*One Tree Hill*), Christopher Shyer (*V*), Terry Serpico (*Army Wives*) and Grant Bowler (*True Blood*).

The DBA webpage is full of information: *www.buchwald.com*.

Agents
David Lewis, Jonathan Mason, Joanne Nici, Ricki Olshan, Rachel Sheedy Alan Willig, Victoria Kress and Pam Goldman
Client List
Vast

✍ Dorothy Palmer Talent Agency ✍

235 W 56th Street, #24K
btwn 7th & 8th Avenues
New York, NY, 10019
212-765-4280

After training with Sol Hurok Enterprises and working with National Concert and Artists Corporation, I guess Dorothy felt ready for anything when she opened her own agency in 1974 and everything is pretty much what she does. In addition to the 14,000 names in her database and 450 pictures in her annual Palmer People Book, she also finds time and energy to cast, produce and package films as well has hand-hold her dozen or so signed clients.

Dorothy's list includes entertainers, actors, writers, producers, broadcasters, comedians, dancers, singers, models, television hosts and hostesses, and senior citizens, many of whom are hyphenates like actor-producer-director Monroe Mann (*You Can't Kill Stephen King*), actress-producer-writer Connie Lamonthe (*Seeking Closure*).

Dorothy also has a literary franchise which will probably benefit her actor clients as well as her screenwriters. Since Dorothy is seriously committed to the plight of independent filmmakers, she is also always looking for investors and has packaged several independent films.

www.dorothypalmertalentagency.com.

Agents
Dorothy Palmer
Client List
A dozen plus freelance

⚹ Fifi Oscard Agency, Inc. ⚹

110 W 40th Street #2100
New York, NY 10018
212-764-1100

The legendary Fifi Oscard died in 2006. A frustrated housewife and mother in 1949 when she began working gratis for Lee Harris Draper, she told me she was inept when she started her job, but quickly became proficient and worked herself up to $15 a week within nine months.

From LHD, Fifi moved to The Lucille Phillips Agency, working three days a week. That inauspicious beginning led to Fifi's purchase of LPA in 1959 and the birth of The Fifi Oscard Agency, Inc.

The agency is now in the hands of managing partner, lit agent Peter Sawyer, and theatrical agent and vice-president, Carmen LaVia. When Carmen came to New York from Las Vegas (with wife Arlene Fontana) looking for a job in the business, he began at an amazing level, lucking into a job as an assistant to legendary producer, Leland Hayward.

When Leland became ill, the office cut back and Carmen joined Fifi. Three years later he joined the William Morris Agency, where he stayed for ten years before coming back home to Fifi.

Carmen is joined by Francis Del Duca who reps for film, television and theatre, Kevin McShane and Jerry Rudes.

Sawyer heads the lit division. His list of best selling authors includes William Shatner, Art Buchwald, William Claxton and Greg Lawrence, who wrote the new Jackie Kennedy bio *Jackie as Editor: The Literary Life of Jacqueline Kennedy Onassis*. FOA also reps directors, producers, singers, composers, and actors. In short, they deal with every aspect of showbiz except the variety field.

Check *www.fifioscard.com* for up-to-date lists of agents and submission guidelines.

Agents
Carmen La Via, Francis Del Duca, Kevin McShane and Jerry Rudes
Client List
Large

⚄ FBI ⚄

Frontier Booking International, Inc.

1560 Broadway
at 46th Street
New York, NY 10036
212-221-0220

When Ian Copeland created FBI in 1979, they were known as one of the largest rock agencies around, ultimately repping Sting, Snoop Doggy Dog, Modern English, and Jane's Addiction, not to mention their very first acting client, Courtney Cox.

Since 1984, when the theatrical department was born, it has become the dominant presence. FBI reps everyone from Broadway (*Billy Elliot, Mary Poppins, etc.*) to the next generation of television stars.

John Shea (SEM&M and Kronick, Kelly & Lauren) heads up the theatrical department representing a hot list of young actors. Clients from that list include Alicia Minshew (*All My Children*), Darien Sills Evans (*Treme, Cosby*), Jacqueline Torres (*FX, Hack*), Sean Nelson (*Fresh, American Buffalo, The Corner*), Coy Stewart (*Are We There Yet*), Maria Lark (*Medium*), Shelly Henning (*Days of Our Lives*), Justin Johnston (*Rent*), Max (*Disney's High School Musical 3*), Steven Lee Merkel (*Nurse Jackie*).

Heather Finn (Abrams Artists) helps John run herd on their talented bunch.

FBI handles all types for all areas. They work with an extensive freelance list in addition to their signed clients. Check out their website: *www.frontierbooking.com*

Agents
John Shea and Heather Finn.
Client List
60 plus freelance

✐ The Gage Group ✐

450 7ᵗʰ Avenue, # 1809
across from Macy's at 34ᵗʰ Street
New York, NY 10036
212-541-5250

The dynamic duo that run The Gage Group New York office, Phil Adelman and Steve Unger, are not only friends, but their backgrounds and personalities are synergistic. A theatre major, Steve taught high school after graduation and was pondering what interesting direction his background might take him. When he found The Gage Group, he knew he was home. Phil was an elementary school teacher, quiz show writer, director, screenwriter, director of musicals and a composer and lyricist. How much better suited could they be?

A successful actor himself, founder Martin Gage worked for Fifi Oscard before opening this agency in 1970. Dynamic, charismatic Martin is headquartered in Los Angeles but spends enough time in NY that he knows all the clients.

Names from the GG list include Harriet Harris, Walter Bobbie, Torah Feldshuh, Debra Monk, Leslie Uggams, Danny Burstein, George Wendt, Darius DeHaas, Mary Testa, Lewis J. Stadlen, Ernie Sabella, Walter Charles, Dee Hoty, John Cunningham, Liz Callaway, Phyllis Newman, Beth Fowler, Chuck Wagner, Becky Ann Baker, Jessica Molaskey and Gary Beach.

Wendie Relkin Adelman heads the commercial/host department.

Agents
Phil Adelman, Steve Unger, Wendie Relkin Adelman and Martin Gage
Client List
65

⪽ The Gersh Agency New York ⪾

41 Madison Ave.
at 26th Street
New York, NY 10010
212-997-1818

GANY was formed when Scott Yoselow, David Guc, Ellen Curren, and Mary Meagher left Don Buchwald & Associates to open a New York office for legendary Los Angeles agent, Phil Gersh.

Yoselow, the sole remaining partner, heads the literary department. Representing the actors are partners Stephen Hirsh (Paradigm) and Rhonda Price along with colleagues Seth Glewen, Jennifer Konawall, Randi Goldstein, Christopher Highland, Jason Gutman and Kyetay Beckner.

The client list shared by The Gersh Agency on both coasts is outstanding and includes John Slattery, Richard Jenkins, Josh Radnor, Mo Rocca, Amanda Peet, J. K. Simmons, Catherine Keener, Jeffrey Demunn, Mary Kay Place, Mena Suvari, Tobey Maguire, Kelli Martin, Gloria Reuben, David Schwimmer, Jane Krakowski, Roma Downey, Victor Garber, Dan Hedaya, Christopher Lloyd, Robert Prosky, and Kyle Secor.

Gersh's already respected literary department was augmented in December 2010 when they acquired prestigious LA lit boutique Hohman Maybank Lieb along with their list of glittering clients.

This agency is meticulous about monitoring new talent by attending showcases and readings. If you don't have a referral, concentrate on doing remarkable work in a showcase and ask them to come and see it.

The Gersh Agency New York also reps directors, authors, and below-the-line clients.

Agents

Scott Yoselow, Stephen Hirsh, Jennifer Konawall, Rhonda Price, Randi Goldstein, Christopher Highland, Jason Gutman, Seth Glewen and Kyetay Beckner

Client List

1979

ᴁ Ginger Dicce Talent Agency ᴂ

56 W 45th Street, #1100
just W of 5th Avenue
New York, NY 10036
212-869-9650

Ginger Dicce has a long memory. When I walked into her office she reminded me that early in our careers, she had cast me in a *Tender Vittles* commercial when she was a commercial producer.

Though I had a tough time getting her on the phone in the first place, Ms. Dicce couldn't have been nicer when we met. Even though she was very busy that day, she still made time to tell me about her business.

One of the few agents in town who still works exclusively freelance, Dicce says she still gives newcomers a chance and looks at every piece of mail that enters her office.

Starting as a secretary in advertising, Ginger moved into production via her smarts and helpful mentors. Once she was producing and casting, she says she fell in love with actors and decided to become an agent.

She started her agency in 1986 and has been busily repping union and non-union actors ever since.

When I asked Ginger what attracted her to an actor she said it was an "inner gut thing," so your guess is as good as mine. Since Ginger suffers no fools, I wouldn't call her unless you are focused, business oriented, and have some idea how you can be marketed.

Agent
Ginger Dicce
Client List
Freelance

☜ Gotham Talent Agency ☞

570 7th Avenue
between 40 and 41st Streets
New York, NY 10018
212-944-8898

I first met Cynthia Katz as a client back in the day when she was starting her career repping kids at Abrams Artists. By the time I was profiling agents, she was heading up the east coast offices of Robert Malcolm's agency, The Artists Group East.

She ran that office for 15 years until November of 2009 when she was conscripted to start Gotham Talent Agency. GTA has managed to survive and prosper in what we all know are difficult show business times.

Clients from her list of about 70 include Tom Hewitt (*Rocky Horror Picture Show*), Michelle Federer (*Wicked*), Phil Burke (*Hell on Wheels*), Robert Lin *(Waiting in Beijing)*.

Agent
Cynthia Katz
Client List
70

✠ Hanns Wolters International ✎

501 Fifth Avenue, #2112A
btwn 2nd & 3rd Avenues
New York, NY 10017
212-714-0100

German talent agent Hanns Wolters finally made it to the US in 1962, after a detour via Israel during WWII, some twenty-five years after his first attempt to escape extermination by Hitler.

Initially specializing in European talent, Hanns soon added a mix of talent. By the seventies HWI was a magnet for commercials.

When his wife, actress Marianne Wolters (Mitzi Bera-Monna), died in the 1990s, one of his German actors, Oliver Mahrdt, became Hanns' unofficial son, helping him not only recover from Marianne's death but also to refocus his business. Oliver, who now owns HWI, ultimately supported Hanns through his own lengthy fatal illness.

The agency is currently experiencing a rebirth of sorts, seeing more actors on Broadway and some of their literary talent represented at Sundance and other film fests.

HWI is still one of the places casting directors call for European actors and is also known for its strong New York character types. Every week you'll see HWI clients on episodic television shot in New York.

Although HWI works with about 300 clients, they say there is a core group of thirty that gets most of the calls. These actors are not only talented but also network and help keep the calls coming in.

This agency doesn't sign contracts with its clients, preferring to work on a handshake basis. They also represent German cinema on the East Coast. Amongst HWI's illustrious projects was Academy Award Best Foreign Language Film winner, *Nowhere in Africa*.

Agent
Oliver Mahrdt
Client List
Freelance/union plus non-union

⚔ Harden-Curtis Associates ⚔

214 W 29th Street, #1203
btwn 7th & 8th Avenue
New York, NY 10001
212-977-8502

In 1996 after fifteen years in the business, Mary Harden and Nancy Curtis opened HCA combining the talents of each into this respected agency. Nancy's MA in advertising from Michigan State University and a childhood spent studying acting give Nancy an acting/marketing background edge few agents possess. Mary Harden's early experiences problem solving with writers and actors in a variety of regional theatre jobs provided her contacts and nurturing skills that pay off for her literary clients.

Before joining HCA in 1997, Diane Riley was in casting at The Roundabout Theatre Company and in company management at the Goodspeed Opera House. Northwestern theatre grad Michael Kirsten came aboard the same year and became a VP in 2009. Scott Edwards, a graduate of the Theatrical Design Department of Texas State University joined the company in 2001. The newest member of the team, Wagner College grad Joanna Bell transformed her internship into a real job when she became a franchised agent in 2008.

Clients include Hunter Bell, Veanne Cox, K Todd Freeman, Anita Gillette, Megan Lawrence, Christiane Noll, Nancy Opel, Hunter Bell, Sarah Botsford, Randy Danson, Lisa Emery, Crystal Dickinson, Damon Gupton, Terrell Tilford, Andrea Anders, Sharon Wilkins, Boris McGiver, Condola Rashad, Brendan Sexton, Alysia Reiner and David Alan Basche. The HC client list includes Tony, Obie, Audelco and NAACP Image awards nominees.

Agents

Nancy Curtis, Mary Harden, Diane Riley, Michael Kirsten, Scott Edwards and Joanna Bell

Client List

150

⋈ Hartig Hilepo Agency ⋉

54 W 21st Street. #610
just W of 5th Avenue
New York, NY 10010
212-929-1772

Paul Hilepo was a student at NYU when he was first exposed to the agency business as an intern at Don Buchwald & Associates. When he graduated in 1992, he sent out resumes to various talent agencies and met and clicked with Michael Hartig. He was a franchised agent two years later.

Hartig established this agency in the early 60s and ran it for forty years until his death in 2004 and now Paul is the new owner.

Liz Rosier joined HH in 2006 from theatre management with both ART and Trinity Rep. Their colleague is New York native, Peter Sanfilippo (Innovative Artists).

HH's impressive list of clients includes Jerry Stiller (*King Of Queens*), Ken Leung (Lost), Phyllis Somerville (*The Big C*), Samrat Chakrabarti (*In Treatment*), Amy Spanger (*Elf*), Lisa Brescia (*Mamma Mia*), Alli Mauzey (*Wicked*), Heidi Schreck (*Circle Mirror Transformation*), Kacie Sheik (*Hair*), Laverne Cox (*Transform Me*), Patti D'arbanville (*Morning Glory*), David Pittu (*Damages*), Tituss Burgess (*30 Rock*), James Saito (Life of Pi) Mousa Kraish (*Do No Harm*) and Jaime Cepero (*Smash*).

Paul says he looks carefully at every picture and resume that comes in, "We can't afford to leave any stone unturned. We find clients in many ways, we check out plays, television shows shooting here, and referrals from people we respect." He says he has found clients from blind submissions.

Agents
Paul Hilepo, Liz Rosier and Peter Sanfilippo
Client List
100

✒ Henderson-Hogan Agency ✒

850 7th Avenue, #1003
btwn 56th & 57th Streets
New York, NY 10019
212-765-5190

Both Maggie Henderson and Jerry Hogan are gone now and the new owner is Jerry's longtime protégée, George Lutsch. George started his career as receptionist-assistant at this iconic bicoastal agency founded by Maggie in 1967.

George's BFA in acting from NYU was the springboard for his first showbiz foray interning with the Royal Court Theatre in London. When he decided to change the direction of his career, he joined Jerry and the rest is history.

George's next in command, Alex Butler, grew up in the city playing guitar and attracted to all things showbiz, so it follows that while he pursued his Philosophy degree from SUNY Purchase, his friends were actors and musicians. After graduation Alex worked briefly at a law firm until his friend George mentioned that he had an opening at HH and Alex finally got into showbusiness where he belonged.

Alex's colleague, Thompson Milam also trained at HH. His BA from the University of Mississippi served him well when he came to the Big City in 2002 and landed his first job at CESD as an assistant after interning at Bernard Telsey Casting. He joined Henderson Hogan in 2008 after a stint as casting director for The Onion News Network. He became franchised at HH in 2011.

Clients from their list include Dakin Matthews (The Fighting Temptations), Peggy Pope (*Law & Order, Ed*), Peter Jay Fernandez (*Cyrano*), Jeremy Bobb (*The Bridge Project*), Christopher Innvar *(The Gershwin's Porgy and Bess)*, David Pegram (*WarHorse*), Joaquina Kalakunga (*Hurt Village*).

Agents
George Lutsch, Alex Butler and Thompson Milam
Client List
100 plus

⚮ ICM Partners ⚮

730 Fifth Avenue
just W of 5th Avenue
New York, NY 10019
212-556-5665

ICM Partners webpage (*www.icmtalent.com*) say it all:

◆ *ICM Partners is one of the world's largest talent and literary agencies with offices in New York, Los Angeles, and London. The agency represents creative and technical talent in the fields of motion picture, television, books, music, live performance, branded entertainment, and new media. ICM was formed in 1975 through the merger of Creative Management Associates and International Famous Agency. In 2005, the company raised equity financing from Rizvi Traverse and institutional investors to fund strategic growth, and in 2006, ICM acquired the literary agency Broder Webb Chervin Silbermann. In 2012, the agency completed a management buyout and formed a partnership with the new name, ICM Partners.*

An article I read said that Traverse was more interested in cost cutting than anything else spurring the partners to take matters into their own hands. The article said the first thing Traverse did was cut the budget for flowers. No wonder the (now) Partners were pissed off!

Although their webpage doesn't mention client names, the television link leads to a long list of television packages including *Modern Family, Dancing with the Stars, Big Bang Theory, Breaking Bad* and many others.

A few of the actor clients from ICM's NY list include Nina Arianda, Alan Arkin, Craig Bierko, Ty Burrell, Bobby Cannavale, Gary Cole, Taye Diggs, Jane Kaczmarek, Eve Best, Kevin Dillon, James Spader, Edie Falco, Gena Rowlands and Vanessa Williams. Check *www.imdbpro.com* for more names of actors and agents.

Agents
Lisa Bankoff, Josh Pearl, Bonnie Bernstein, Sean Liebowitz, Josh Pearl, Zach Iser, Steven Fisher, Phil Sutfin, Paul Martino and Adam Schweitzer
Client List
2023

▵ Ingber & Associates ▵

1140 Broadway, # 907
btwn 26th & 27th Streets
New York, NY 10001
212-889-9450

Carole Ingber worked in motion picture advertising before moving to Los Angeles to work in casting with Vicki Rosenberg in 1982. Since returning from the West Coast, she has worked at a succession of high profile commercial agencies: J. Michael Bloom, SEM&M, LW2 and headed the commercial division of Susan Smith's distinguished agency before opening her own office in 1993.

Although I&A is a commercial agency, I include them because they specialize in handling commercial careers of working actors. Carole may be the woman to talk to if you are already working good jobs as an actor and are looking for someone to handle the commercial part of your business.

Agents
Carole Ingber
Client List
250 plus freelance

◢ Innovative Artists ◣

235 Park Avenue South
btwn 19th & 20th Streets
New York, NY 10003
212-253-6900

In 1982 Gersh alum Scott Harris arrived on the agency scene in Los Angeles. Evolving through various partnerships, his agency now has offices in New York, Chicago and two in Santa Monica, California. A prestigious boutique agency from the get-go, the agency has now grown into one of the most important independent agencies on either coast giving ICM, WME and UTA a run for their money with a client list that totals 2838 and a staff of 63.

The New York office is in the capable hands of Gary Gersh along with colleagues Brian Davidson and Ken Lee (who began his career at Innovative). Lisa Lieberman (ICM), Allison Levy (Ambrosio Mortimer), and Bill Veloric (Peter Strain and Associates) join them in repping Hank Azaria (*Love and Other Drugs*), Irfan Khan (*In Treatment, The Namesake*), Cynthia Nixon (*Sex & the City*), Amanda Seyfried (*Red Riding Hood*), Corey Parker (*The End of the Bar*), Kate Nelligan (*Cider House Rules*), Patti LuPone (*Summer of Sam*), Traci Lords (*First Wave*), Joel Grey (*Cabaret*), Jason Alexander (*Seinfeld*), Swoozie Kurtz (*Mike & Molly*), F. Murray Abraham (*Amadeus*), Adam Storke (*Over There*) and many others.

Jaime Misher and Dannielle Quinoa shepherd Innovative's Young Adult and Kids division while Maury DiMauro helms one of New York's largest Beauty and Print divisions.

Clients are seen at this agency strictly by referral.

Agents
Gary Gersh, Brian Davidson, Ken Lee, Lisa Lieberman, Allison Levy, Bill Veloric, Jaime Misher, Dannielle Quinoa, Maury DiMauro
Client List
2838

✑ Jim Flynn, Inc. ✍

307 W 38ᵗʰ Street, #801
New York, NY 10018
212-868-1068

Jim Flynn entered show business in 1990 answering phones at Susan Smith's agency. His first agenting job was at the New York Agency which merged with Alliance Talent. In 1995 he and Judy Boals came together to create Berman, Boals & Flynn, one of the most effective talent and literary agencies in town. At that time they were partnered with literary icon Lois Berman.

In the spring of 2003, after seven years as partners, Judy and Jim mutually decided they wanted their own agencies. Since they were friends, they decided to share space. Even when Judy moved a block west, Jim ended up moving to the same building on the same floor. Old bonds continue.

Somehow Jim has managed to maintain a successful talent/literary agency and attend law school at the same time. In 2003 he earned the right to sign "Esq." after his name. As a lawyer he can add entertainment law to his list of services, a big plus for clients. Flynn's list of actors includes Frank Wood and Enid Graham.

His clients come mostly through referrals. Although this office looks at all pictures and resumes, they rarely call anyone in from them.

Agents
Jim Flynn
Client List
30

⚓ Jordon Gill & Dornbaum Agency ⚓

1133 Broadway, #623
at 26th Street
New York, NY 10010
212-463-8455

Although Robin Dornbaum loved actors and wanted to work with them some way, she never knew how until she interned with the legendary Marje Fields while still in school as a communications major. At that point Robin knew she had found her calling. After six months, mentor Fields sent her to work in casting at Reed Sweeney Reed, where she worked for free, honed her skills, stored information and grew in the business. After graduation, she got a job at The Joe Jordon Agency.

Within three years Robin was President and brought in Jeffrey Gill (Bonni Kidd, Fifi Oscard) as her partner. Their combination of youth, savvy, and industriousness changed this agency into one of the top child and young adult agencies in New York.

Former actor David McDermott (FBI, HWA) reps the eighteen to thirty age group and is interested in special skills (skateboarders, all types of athletes, dancers, little people, beatboxers, etc.). Jeff heads the legit department, while Robin reps the commercial clients.

Clients include Katrina Bowden (*Rock, Nurse 3D, American Reunion*), Ruby Jerins (*Nurse Jackie, Shutter Island, Remember Me*), Sterling Jerins (*The Warren Files, World War Z*), Matt Bush (*High School-The Movie, Piranha 3DD, Trouble with the Curve*), Olivia Thirlby (*Juno, No Strings Attached, The Darkest Hour, Dredd*), Erin Moriarty (*The Watch, The Philosophers, ABC's The Red Widow*), Julia Goldani Telles (*ABC Family's Bunheads*), Jonny Weston (*Of Men and Mavericks, Cherry, Someday This Pain Will be Useful to You*), Suzanne and Colleen Dengel (*The Devil Wears Prada, Plus One*), Charlie Kilgore (*Moonrise Kingdom*), Byrant Price (*The Lone Ranger*), Ian Nelson (*The Hunger Games*). Check out *www.jgdtalent.com* for more info.

Agents
Robin Dornbaum, Jeffrey Gill, and David McDermott
Client List
50-60

✄ Judy Boals, Inc. ✄

307 W 30th Street, #812
New York, NY 10018
212-500-1424

Judy Boals started in the business as an actor, but a part-time job working in varying capacities with literary legend Lois Berman ultimately led not only to her agenting career, but also to a partnership with Berman and talent/literary agent Jim Flynn (Susan Smith, The New York Agency, Alliance Talent) in 1995.

Berman died in January of 2003 and that spring, after seven years as partners, Boals and Flynn mutually decided they wanted their own agencies. But since they were friends, they decided to share space.

Names from Judy's list include, Peggy Shaw, Klea Blackhurst, David Mogentale, David Greenspan, Daren Kelly and Katherine Helmond.

Boals continues to represent actors, composers/songwriters, directors and writers who are chosen not only for their talent, but because they are easy to get along with.

Agents
Judy Boals
Client List
50

✍ Kazarian, Spencer, Ruskin & Associates ✉

Media Arts Building
311 W 43rd Street
btwn 7th and 8th Avenues
New York, NY 10017
212-582-7572

While training in the Graduate Acting Program at NYU, Lori Swift discovered her desire to advocate for actors. In 1996, she made the transition into casting at Bernard Telsey. Six years later when Los Angeles powerhouse KSR decided to open a legit office in New York, they tapped the Telsey casting veteran for the job. Lori brought her vast amount of experience from both acting and casting along with her professional relationships to help build a theatrical division.

Lori is joined by colleague Danielle Quinoa (Innovative Artists) representing a distinguished list that includes Glenn Fleshler *(Boardwalk Empire, Margaret, Death of A Salesman)*, Tonya Pinkins *(Milk Like Sugar, Storefront Church, Newlyweeds)*, J. Robert Spencer *(Next To Normal, Jersey Boys)*, Anneliese Van Der Pol *(That's So Raven, Vampires Suck)*, Amanda Perez *(Gossip Girl, Don John's Addiction)*, Seth Kirschner *(30 Rock, Hannah Has A Ho Phase)*, Bryce Ryness *(Hair, Leap of Faith)*, Jessica Stone *(Greetings From Tim Buckley, Anything Goes)*, Susie Pourfar *(Tribes, The Good Wife)*, Saycon Sengbloh *(Fela!, Hurt Village)*, PJ Griffith *(The Dark Knight Rises, Giant)*, Christy Altomare *(Carrie, Spring Awakening)*, Karl Kenzler *(House of Cards, Mary Poppins)*, Ilana Levine *(Imogene, Friends With Kids, Greetings From Tim Buckley)*, Kamahl Naiqui *(Da Brick, Gossip Girl)*, Martha Millan *(Entourage, Falling For Grace)*, Ben Platt *(Pitch Perfect)*.

Agents
Lori Swift and Danielle Quinoa
Client List
80

⚞ Kerin-Goldberg Associates ⚟

155 E 55th Street, #5D
btwn 3rd & Lexington Avenues
New York, NY 10022
212-838-7373

Charles Kerin's interest in the business was so strong that in his first job as a publicist for *Scholastic Magazine*, he convinced management to create a film award just so he could get to see free movies. His first agent job was with the prestigious Coleman-Rosenberg agency.

Charles left C-R to open his own literary agency representing soap writers in 1985. Partner Ellie Goldberg was an actress when old school chum Gary Epstein cajoled her into joining his office and becoming an agent. Goldberg's path has also included stints with Henderson-Hogan, Bonni Allen and ultimately, Coleman-Rosenberg. Although Charles was working at another agency when he was called on to broker a literary deal for one of C-R's theatrical clients, he and Ellie hit it off immediately and spoke often of opening their own agency when the time was right.

1995 turned out to be the magic year when Kerin and Goldberg got together to create this classy agency representing actors, playwrights, directors, composers, choreographers, songwriters, scenic designers, costume designers, and art directors.

Ellie, Charles and colleague Ron Ross (Waters Nicolosi) represent an impressive list that features Jean Stapleton and Donald Sadler, among others. They see new clients only by referral but do look at all pictures and resumes.

There are incisive comments from Ellie elsewhere in the book. Be sure to check them out.

Agents
Charles Kerin, Ellie Goldberg and Ron Ross
Client List
100

◈ The Krasny Office, Inc. ◈

1501 Broadway
btwn 43rd & 44th Streets
New York, NY 10019
212-730-8160

Gary Krasny has a valuable background for an agent. He was an actor, a publicist for Berkeley Books, a story editor for Craig Anderson (after he left the Hudson Theatre Guild), and an assistant to Broadway general manager Norman Rothstein at Theatre Now. In 1985 he decided he was more empathetic with the artist than management and decided to become an agent.

Gary honed his agenting skills at various agencies before opening his own in late 1991. He found office space not only in the same building, but on the same floor where he had worked with Craig Anderson years before.

Gary's background, experience and taste made him a favorite with the casting community. When he opened his office, he quickly became part of the mainstream.

Gary runs the legit department along with colleague B. Lynne Jebens (Michael Hartig) and the new addition to their office, Chris Nichols (Kerin-Goldberg). Gary says "Chris brings a new energy to Krasnyland as well as a very solid musical department."

Clients from their list include Denny Dillon (*Dream On*), Meg Mundy and Ken Jennings.

The Krasny Office has liaison arrangements with several Los Angeles agents and managers.

Agents
Gary Krasny, B. Lynne Jebens and Chris Nichols
Client List
105

⊲ Leading Artists, Inc. ⊳

145 W 45ᵗʰ Street, #1000
btwn 6ᵗʰ & Broadway Avenues
New York, NY 10036
212-391-4545

Owner Dianne Busch came to New York from Ohio in 1979 figuring to act, but soon found a cross-section of showbiz jobs she liked, ranging from casting commercials with Joy Weber to legit with Meg Simon. A brief stint as a manager led the way to agenthood at Silver, Massetti and Szatmary in 1991.

When Monty Silver retired 12 years later, Dianne bought the agency and changed the name to Leading Artists, Inc.

Working with Dianne are Michael Kelly Boone and Diana Doussant (Talentworks). They oversee the careers of clients Zeljko Ivanek (*The Event, Damages*), Gregory Jbara *(Blue Bloods, Billy Elliot)*, James Rebhorn (*Homeland, White Collar, 12 Angry Men*), Richard Masur (*Girls*), Adriane Lenox (*Doubt, The Blind Side*), Afton Williamson (*Homeland, A Gifted Man*), Jayne Houdyshell (*Follies, Well, Wicked*), Brooks Ashmanskas (*Promises, Promises*), Daniel Jenkins (*Billy Elliot*), Eisa Davis (*Hart of Dixie, Passing Strange*), A.J. Shively (*February House*), Larry Pine (*Homeland*), Rosie Benton (*Stickfly*), Teresa Avia Lim *(Water By The Spoonful)*, Uzo Aduba (*Godspell*), David Gregory (*How Do You Know?*), Andy Groteluschen (*Taming of the Shrew*), Jessie Austrian (*Cymbeline*), Ivan Hernandez (*Into The Woods*), Chuck Cooper and Aaron Schwartz (both of *Gossip Girl*), Jonathan Dent and Lizbeth MacKay (both in *Sons of the Prophet*), Brendan Griffin (*Clybourne Park*), Finnerty Steeves *(Smash, Lost In Yonkers)*, Marceline Hugot (*30 Rock*), Fyvush Finkel (*Nixon, Harry's Law*), Rashidra Scott (*Sister Act*) and Bill Army (*Relatively Speaking*).   Leading Artists is affiliated with Los Angeles agencies SMS Talent and SDB Partners.

Agents
Dianne Busch, Michael Kelly Boone and Diana Doussant
Client List
150

⋈ Luedeke Agency ⋈

1674 Broadway, #7A
btwn 52nd & 53rd Streets
New York, NY 10019
212-765-9564

Penny Luedeke has been in some kind of showbiz related job since she was twelve, but her entrance into the agency business came because she is such a stalwart friend. When an acquaintance who owned a classical music management company asked her to run his office for a few weeks while he was in Europe on business, Penny demurred at first, but finally acquiesced and was surprised by how much she enjoyed the work.

To learn the agency business, she approached children's agent Pat Gilchrist in 1996 about starting an adult department at her agency.

When Penny opened her own office a year later, her multi-talented friends all wanted to be clients so she determined to represent not only actors, but writers and directors as well.

Penny is now joined by colleague Barbara Feinstein.

Penny looks carefully at all pictures and resumes and has found a couple of her most successful clients that way.

Agents
Penny Luedeke and Barbara Feinstein
Client List
50

⩗ LTA ⩘

Lally Talent Agency
Film Center Building
630 9th Avenue, #800
at 44th Street
New York, NY 10038
212-974-8718

Dale Lally was an actor and personal manager before he crossed the desk to become an agent. He worked for Mary Ellen White and Nobel Talent before partnering with print agents Wallace Rogers and Peter Lerman (Lally Rogers & Lerman).

When Lally, Rogers and Lerman decided to go their separate ways in 1992, Dale opened this office.

Partner Stephen Laviska worked in contract law before he joined Dale in representing their strong list of musical performers, interesting young adults, and solid character people.

Actors from their list include Brad Oscar, James Lally, Angel Caban, Alice Spivak, Jerome Preston Bates, Tibor Feldman, David Lipman, Capathia Jenkins and Aisha de Haas.

Agents
Dale Lally and Stephen Laviska
Client List
45

﹥ Nicolosi & Co. Inc. ﹤

150 W 25th Street, #1200
btwn 6th & 7th Avenues
New York, NY 10001
212-633-1010

After getting a B.A. in acting from U Mass and an MA in both acting and directing from Emerson College, Jeanne Nicolosi taught acting and headed the theatre department at a Boston high school. She moved to New York in the late 70s to act and direct and though she found success at both, she wanted more control over her career and to coach and develop others. Her first exposure as an assistant agent with Beverly Anderson convinced her she was on that path.

In 1985 Jeanne became a franchised agent, working briefly at Writers & Artists before joining The Bob Waters Agency where she continued to hone her talent and business management skills and was promoted to partner. Gradually envisioning her own agency, Nicolosi's dream was realized in 2002 when she opened Nicolosi & Company, Inc. She met all her first year goals and now eight years later, she continues to grow.

Ex-thesp, David Cash (Henderson/Hogan, CESD, Harter Manning Woo) and Jeremy Leiner join Jeanne in repping her impressive list of actors for Broadway, film and television. Names from her list include Caissie Levy (*Hair, Ghost*), Julia Murney (*Wicked*), Mariann Mayberry (*Steppenwolf*), J. Elaine Marcos (*Morning Glory, Priscilla*), Sara Gettelfinger (*Dirty Rotten Scoundrels, Free Man of Color*), Jonny Orsini (*Generation Um*), James Chen (*L&O: SVU*), Jenny Powers (*Grease*), Jennifer Lim (*Chinglish*), Lucy Walters (*Shame, 666 Park*), Marina Squerciati (*Gossip Girl*), Joe Forbrich (*L&O*), and two new stars to be Greg Perri and Jason Ralph.

Agents
Jeanne Nicolosi, David Cash and Jeremy Leiner
Client List
100

✦ Meg Pantera, The Agency ✦

138 W 15th Street, First Floor
btwn 6th and 7th Avenues
New York City, NY 10011
212-219-9330

Meg Pantera was the artistic director at Buffalo's The Theatre Of Youth Company and also at the Rochester Association of Performing Arts before she followed a new love to the Big Apple in 1990. A friend suggested she would make a good agent so she signed on for a part time stint with Bob Barry (Barry Haft Brown) and was franchised five years later. She opened her own agency in January 2000.

Meg feels the partnership between an actor and an agent is forged by mutual hard work and respect. In a time when boutique agencies are failing, hers thrives. She says she prizes the close relationships she has developed with her clients helping them develop their careers.

Clients include Drew Sarich premiering in Germany as Rocky in *Rocky the New Musical*, Paul Whitty (*Once*), Brian J. Keane (*War Horse, Lights Out*), Kenita Miller (*Once on this Island, Color Purple*), Geno Segers (*Pair of Kings*), Nathan Lee Graham (*Priscilla Queen of the Desert, Wild Party, Sweet Home Alabama, Zoolander*), Patricia Buckley (*Evolution*), Abigail Savage (*Precious*), Ramsey Farallagallah (*Homeland*), Zainab Jah (*The Convert*), and actor-director-respected teacher of Michael Chekhov technique, Lenard Petit.

Meg attends showcases, readings and accepts headshots by mail.

Agent
Meg Pantera
Client List
75

⚘ Paradigm ⚘

360 Park Avenue South, 16th Floor
at 26th Street
New York, NY 10110
212-897-6400

Once thought of as a baby conglomerate, Paradigm now has more clients and more staff than UTA. Created from the 1992 merger of two elegant talent agencies, Los Angeles' Gores/Fields and New York's STE (Clifford Stevens), along with uber LA lit agencies, Robinson/Weintraub & Gross, and Shorr Stille & Associates, Paradigm has offices in New York, Los Angeles, Nashville and Monterey, California.

Paradigm guides the careers of an elite roster of actors, musical artists, directors, writers, and producers. Led by chairman Sam Gores, the agency continues to grow and prosper.

Names from Paradigm's prestigious list include Michael Gambon, James Earl Jones, Andy Garcia, Philip Seymour Hoffman, Denis Leary, Neil Patrick Harris, Katherine Heigl, Allan Arkush, William Baldwin, Charles Durning, Simon Callow, Campbell Scott, Laurence Fishburne, Eli Wallach, Anne Jackson, Dana Ivey, Max Van Sydow, Allison Janney, Chris Cooper and Dennis Franz.

Broadcast bigwig Jim Griffin (WMA) joined the agency in early 2010 to create Paradigm's broadcasting department bringing along longtime clients Regis Philbin, Emeril Lagasse, Jim Lehrer, Chris Cuomo, Geraldo Rivera, John Gibson, Bernard Goldberg, Mike Barnicle, Fred Thompson, Charles Grodin and Willard Scott.

Offices in Nashville and Monterey rep their music stars.

Agents

Clifford Stevens, Richard Schmenner, Matthew Smith, Erin Castellanos, Sarah Fargo, Fred Hashagen, Christopher Highland, Kevin Kastrup, Ed Micone, Jonathan Mills, Tim Sage

Client List

2124

✑ Peggy Hadley Enterprises ✍

250 W 57ᵗʰ Street, #2317
btwn 7ᵗʰ & 8ᵗʰ Avenues
New York, NY 10107
212-246-2166

Another actor who changed sides of the desk, Peggy Hadley has never missed performing. When she was searching for a new career, fellow performer Fannie Flagg talked Peggy into becoming her manager. Peggy managed Fannie and four others until their careers drew them west. Peggy (a transplanted Kentuckian) felt she couldn't bear leaving the city to go with them to Los Angeles, so she just added more actors to her list and became an agent.

She has about sixty to seventy signed clients and works with many others freelance. She handles only legit, no commercials.

Clients from her list include Lou Meyers, Clifford David, and Danette Holden (*Laughing Room Only, The Sound of Music, Shrek*).

Agent
Peggy Hadley
Client List
50

◣ Peter Strain & Associates ◢

321 W 44th St. # 805
btwn 8th & 9th Avenues
New York, NY 10036
212-391-0380

When Bill Timms arrived in the city in 1984 to pursue an acting career, he found that though his community theatre background helped him get some auditions, it didn't insulate him from the pain that follows. Rejected after four callbacks for a coveted job, he presented himself to his agent at Writers & Artists saying he felt he would be more successful on the other side of the desk. From W&A he went to The NY Agency, Sames & Rollnick and the Tantleff Office before joining Strain in 2000. The Scranton native has helmed Peter Strain & Associates since 1985 when Strain moved west to open the Los Angeles division.

Colleague Jeffrey Lockhorn received his BA from NYU in Dramatic Literature and was an assistant at Paradigm before arriving at PSA in 2007 and becoming franchised soon after.

Frankie Moran was a musical theatre performer and graduate of UCLA's School of Theater, Film and Television before working as a theatre critic in outlets including *Back Stage* and *www.sandiego.com* as a member of the San Diego Theatre Critics Circle. After moving to New York, Frankie cut his teeth assisting at Dave Clemmons Casting and Telsey + Co, and became the newest agent at Peter Strain in 2011.

A few clients from their combined east and west coast client list are Nick Spangler (*Book of Mormon*), Adam Jacobs (*The Lion King*), James Lescene (*The Best Man*), Molly Ranson (*Jerusalem and Carrie*), Terence Archie *(The Elaborate Entrance of Chad Diety)*, Rene Auberjonois (*Boston Legal*), Jonathan Hadary (*Gypsy, Spamalot*) and Erin Krakow (*Army Wives*).

Agents
Bill Timms, Jeffrey Lockhorn and Frankie Moran
Client List
90

◢ Phoenix Artists ◣

330 W 39th Street, # 607
btwn 8th and 9th Avenues
New York, NY 10018
212-586-9110

When Gary Epstein was in the 4th grade, Mary Martin was starring on Broadway in the *Sound of Music*. Seeking an audition so that her son might follow in her footsteps, Gary's pro-active-singer mom wrote Martin and an audition was arranged. Gary said the stage manager actually said to him, "don't call us, we'll call you".

They never called, but Gary immediately started studying acting and performing in local and children's theatre companies. He interrupted his studies as a drama major at Hofstra University for a year to work in Hollywood for Eli Landau's *American Film Theatre*.

After graduation, though he landed some acting jobs, when his friend arranged a day job with the Mort Schwartz Agency, Gary's future was set. He worked for Mort for a year before joining legendary NY agent Stark Hesseltine (Hesseltine-Baker) in 1978. When Baker died in 1986, Gary opened Phoenix Artists.

In 1991 seeking a bicoastal presence, Gary began a long partnership with Los Angeles agent Craig Wyckoff (Epstein/Wyckoff and later Epstein Wyckoff Corsa Ross & Associates).

That partnership dissolved in 2005 and Phoenix Artists rose again. Veteran Randi Ross continues with Gary along with newly minted agent, Justin Busch. Phoenix is primarily a theatrical agency servicing actors in all parts of the business. They have a small literary list of writers and directors, all either old friends or actor clients who became hyphenates and asked Gary to shepherd their careers.

Agents
Gary Epstein, Randi Ross and Justin Busch
Client List
20

✄ The Price Group Talent ✄

155 Avenue of the Americas, 6th floor
at Spring Street
New York, NY 10013
212 725-1980

After graduating SUNY Purchase with a Dramatic Arts Degree and an interest in production, Lisa Price moved to San Diego to intern at San Diego Rep. There she cast, directed and assisted both Josephina Lopez on the first production of *Real Women Have Curves* and the theatre's founder and Artistic Director, Sam Woodhouse. She has since cast, acted, directed and produced for a variety of television and theatre projects in both Los Angeles and New York.

A friend's suggestion led Lisa in a new direction to an ad on *www.playbill.com* for an assistant with iconic talent agent, Beverly Anderson. Anderson recognized Lisa's inherent skills, taught her the agency business and encouraged her to be an agent almost immediately. Price left Anderson in 2006 to open her own agency.

Her clients work Broadway, film, television, national tours, commercials, the web and Vegas. Names from her list include Allen Louis Rickman (*A Serious Man, Boardwalk Empire, You Don't Know Jack*), and Shayna Steele (*Rent, Hairspray, Sex And The City 2*). Shayna is also the lead singer for Moby and part of Bette Midler's *The Showgirl Must Go On* in Las Vegas. Lisa now also represents supermodel, Claudia Mason as well as actress and LML recording artist, Tamela D'Amico.

Price judges talent competitions, attends showcases and gives seminars with an eye for new talent to add to her select list. She only reps talent age 18 and over. Her website is *www.thepricegrouptalent.com*.

Agent
Lisa Price
Client List
30

⫸ Professional Artists ⫷

321 W 44th Street, #605
btwn 8th & 9th Avenues
New York, NY 10036
212-247-8770

Sheldon Lubliner is fun, easy to talk to, informed, a good negotiator and he has a good client list. Add charm, taste, ability, access and his great partner Marilynn Scott Murphy, and you've pretty much got a picture of Professional Artists.

As a director-producer Sheldon enjoyed all the details involved in mounting shows for Al Pacino, Gene Barry, and Vivica Lindfors; he just didn't like raising the money.

Deciding he could transfer all his skills into agenting and not be a fundraiser, Sheldon changed careers in 1980, translating his contacts and style into an agency called News and Entertainment. PA is an outgrowth of that venture.

Actress/client Marilynn Scott Murphy was commandeered to answer phones in a pinch in 1984, and in 1987 became a co-owner of PA. Having been a successful actress herself, Marilynn brought with her people skills and knowledge necessary to successfully represent actors in this highly competitive industry.

In 2005 Ashley Williams joined the agency having finished graduate school at the National Theatre Conservatory. Starting as an assistant she quickly became a franchised agent within the office, bringing with her intelligence and humor. Their list includes not only actors, news and radio personalities, but also writers, producers, directors, and casting directors.

Agents
Sheldon Lubliner, Marilynn Scott and Ashley Williams
Client List
100

✄ The Roster Agency ✄

247 W 38th St, 10th Fl
Btwn 7th and 8th Avenues
New York, NY 10018
212-725-8459

Michael Rodriguez (Hartig Hilipo, DGRW) and I were unable to ever get together for this profile, but I wanted to add him to the book anyway, so my sources were all online starting with an April 2011 profile at *www.actorsconnection.com* and general information from *www.imdbpro.com*.

I look forward to finally speaking with Michael because the article says that Michael's first agency was called Ugly Talent. I don't know what his client list looked like then, but today's list doesn't seem at all ugly: Didi Conn (*Grease*), John Amos (*Madea's Witness Protectin*), Tina Louise (*The Stepford Wives*), Susan Anton (*Baywatch*), Diane Salinger (*Carnivale*) and John Rubinstein (*Atlas Shrugged: Part 2*).

I don't know when he opened The Roster Agency, but his website copywrite date is 2009. *www.therosteragency.com*.

Agent
Michael Rodriguez
Client List
50

⊠ Sheplin - Winik Artists ⊠

676A 9th Avenue
Box 164
New York City, NY 10036
646-246-8853

Sue Winik comes from a three generation showbiz family. Her mom was Edger Bergen's protégée, Sue was an actor and so was her son from age seven until college.

Since Sue has been and actor, a manager and an agent, she brings a wide vision to her select group of clients.

Originally partnered with H. Shep Pamplin when they created the agency in 2005, when Shep moved to Oklahoma to teach and run a theatre, Sue decided to run SWA on her own.

She reps young comedians, adults and young adults who work tours, sketch comedy, regional theatre, television and Broadway.

Clients include Jack Haley (*Boardwalk Empire*), Christine Dwyer (*Wicked*), "Ellie" Meyer (*Boardwalk Empire*), Suzanne Smart (*Guilty*) and Kent Jackman (*Law & Order: SVU*).

Sue says a sense of humor is a must for her clients.

Agent
Sue Winik
Client List
Freelance

◁ Stone Manners Salners ▷

900 Broadway, #910
btwn 19th & 20th Streets
New York, NY 10003
212-505-1400

The offspring of a famous British agent, Tim Stone came to Los Angeles in 1979 to provide services for British actors in this country by establishing his own agency, UK Management. Although he used his British list as a base in the beginning, Tim's list quickly expanded to represent a much broader base.

By 1982 Tim had acquired partner Larry Masser (Stone Masser), and by April 1986 Scott Manners' (Fred Amsel, Richard Dickens Agency) name was added to the masthead (Stone Manners Masser). Larry left the following August, but since then, Tim and Scott's partnership has prevailed.

In January 2003, at a time when many NYC agencies were closing, Stone Manners was doing so well that they decided to open an East Coast office. Tim moved to Manhattan and Scott keeps the business in tact in Los Angeles.

After a career as a child actor, Ohio colleague Ben Sands (The Mine) enrolled at Boston University where his eyes were opened to the many opportunities in showbusiness that existed other than acting. Upon graduation in 2003, his new consciousness led to a series of internships that brought him a new life as a franchised agent. Sands joined SMS in 2011.

SMS won't let me name anyone from their list of actors, directors, producers, scriptwriters, young adults, and teens, so you'll have to check *www.imdbpro.com* for that information.

Agents
Tim Stone and Ben Sands
Client List
They won't say

☒ Stewart Talent ☒

318 W 53rd St, Ste 201
between 8th & 9th Avenues
New York, NY 10019
212 315 5505

Chicago agent Jane Stewart created her signature agency in 1980 with a staff of two. Today her empire includes agencies in New York (2004) and in Atlanta (2010) and her staff has grown to twenty.

Her New York partner, Don Birge was originally an actor who much preferred scoring the job, not working it. It finally occurred to him that agenting would multiply his pleasure at job getting without the drawback of actually having to act. He interned at a couple of NY agencies before joining with Stewart to open their Manhattan office in November of 2004. Since the roots of this distinguished agency are in Chicago, the client list is heavy with Chicago talent that includes *August: Osage County* standouts Rondi Reed and Deanna Dunagan.

Don's colleagues have varied backgrounds. He says he "stole Kara Volkmann from her wardrobe career" to help him open the agency, while Scott Tanzer worked at Warner Bros. and Steve Maihack was at Don Buchwald Associates. They rep an amazing list that includes Betty Buckley, Nora Dunn, Carol Kane, Daniel J. Travanti, Rose Hemingway, Rusty Schwimmer and Stephen Wallem. You can see all their clients and their pictures at *www.stewarttalent.com/newyork*.

Agents
Don Birge, Scott Tanzer, Steve Maihack, Kara Volkmann
Client List
200

☙ The Talent House ❧

325 W 38th Street # 605
btwn 8th and 9th Avenues
New York, NY 10018
212-957-5220

Toronto based, Bruce Dean's Talent House established a New York presence in 1999 and is today helmed by Pete Kaiser (The Gage Group, Henderson-Hogan). Originally an actor, Pete's day job as a bookkeeper at The Gage Group quickly became more interesting than pursuing an acting career so when a full-time job opened up, he switched sides of the desk and quickly became franchised. Though he relocated to the Los Angeles office in 2002, he couldn't stay away from the Big Apple. He joined Talent House in 2008 where he is joined by colleague Jed Abrahams (Henderson-Hogan, Stewart Talent) in repping an impressive boutique list of actors.

A few from their list are Todd Buonopane (*30 Rock*), Bailey Buntain (*Bunheads*), Alison Frasier (*The Secret Garden*), Donna Lynne Champlin (*Sweeney Todd*), Jennifer Cody (*The Princess and the Frog*), Lusia Strus (*Restless*), Matt McGrath (*Boys Don't Cry*), Henriette Mantel (*Grownups*), Josh Young (*Jesus Christ Superstar*), Emily Skinner (*Side Show*), Bailey Buntain (*Bunheads*) and Jeremy Kushnier (*Footloose, Jersey Boys*).

Agents
Pete Kaiser and Jed Abrahams
Client List
90

⊠ The Mine ⊠

347 W 36th Street
btwn 8th & 9th Avenues
New York NY 10018
212-612-3200

David Crombie's tech marketing background seems diametrically opposed to showbusiness, but when friends persuaded him to move to Los Angeles in 2000 to learn the agency business, it turned out that he had a knack for it. After a year's training, he moved to New York and spent six years building his powers and contacts before hiring legit powerhouses David Krasner (Penny Leudeke) to join him creating The Mine in 2007.

Krasner who runs the legit division, grew up in the city eternally fascinated by all things showbiz. After graduating from Binghamton with a degree in English Literature, he was a casting intern at Telsey + Company.

Dustin Flores was head of the musical theatre department at Judy Boals, Inc. before joining the Mine. He joins David repping a client list that includes Marla Mindelle (*Sister Act*), Jeff Kready (*Billy Elliot*), Rachel Potter (*Evita, The Adams Family*), Trista Moldovan (*Phantom of the Opera*), Rachel Bay Jones (*Women on the Verge of a Nervous Breakdown*), Will Connolly (*Once*), Nic Rouleau (*Book of Mormon*) and Ryan Steele (*Newsies the Musical, Billy Elliot*).

Clients mostly come to this agency via referral.

Agents
David Krasner, David Crombie and Dustin Flores
Client List
90

✍ Talent Representatives, Inc. ✍

1040 First Avenue
btwn 56th & 57th Streets
New York, NY 10022
212-752-1835

Honey Raider and Steve Kaplan's mutual love of theatre, film, and television led them to create this agency as a way to become involved in show business. Steve died many years ago, but Honey has managed to survive and prosper on her own. In fact, in 2011 Talent Representatives entered its 47th year!

Honey maintains a limited list of actors in order to ensure a personal approach. Though the agency was created to represent actors, Honey says many of her actor clients who worked daytime shows decided to write and ended up being staff writers and ultimately producers, so she became their lit agent as well. She is joined by colleague Kelly Stark.

Talent Representatives is now one of the few agencies that has a real daytime television literary business. Honey's list of clients is confidential.

Agent
Honey Raider and Kelly Stark
Client List
17 plus freelance

⚔ Talentworks New York ⚖

505 Eighth Avenue
btwn 35th and 36th Streets
New York, NY 10018
212-889-0800

Jay Kane had stars in his eyes when he arrived in New York to study with Stella Adler at NYU, but after graduation, he assessed his acting range and began searching for another theatre career path.

The search took him to New Hampshire's Hampton Playhouse where he grew from teenage apprentice to perennial summer general company and/or stage manager. In the winter he returned to NY, still searching for his place in the business. Working as a business manager at the WPA, as an AD on a Broadway show, and several years in ticket sales at the Metropolitan Opera, Kane turned a deaf ear to friends who kept telling him he'd make a great agent, but in 1990 he embraced his destiny by taking a receptionist job at Select Artists and starting up the ladder. Just three years later he was an agent at The Tantleff Office and in 1998 he joined the original owner of Talentworks, Patty Woo.

Woo is now a manager in Los Angeles and Talentworks belongs to Jay, whose varied showbiz resume makes him an empathetic and business savvy partner.

Jay's list is ever impressive and includes Joe Morton (*Bounce*), Karen Ziemba (*Contact*), Carolyn McCormick (*Law & Order*), Michael Berresse, Ian Kahn, Peter Riegert (*Damages*), Robert Cuccioli (*Jeckyll & Hyde*), Amy Irving *(Carrie, Coast of Utopia),* and Elie Wallach (*Studio 60 on the Sunset Strip*).

Agents
Jay Kane
Client List
250 combined coasts

◁ WME ▷

William Morris Endeavor

1325 Avenue of the Americas
btwn 53rd and 54th Streets
New York, NY 10019
212-903-1100

The agency created by Mr. William Morris in 1898 is no more. In the great Endeavor-William Morris merger of 2009, though Endeavor settled for last billing, they pretty much took everything else. Of the three co-CEOs running the place, two are from Endeavor (Ari Emanuel and Patrick Whitesell) and one from WMA (Dave Wirtschafter) so it's easy to see that the 14-year-old upstart Endeavor Agency pretty much told the 111 year old agency how it was going to be.

After the shift, many agents and stars were displaced, but the fall out has been minimal. The word is that the agency runs well and that team spirit runs rampant.

A few from WME's glittering client list of 2727 are Tina Fey, Steve Carrell, Amy Adams, Aaron Sorkin, Denzel Washington, Ryan Reynolds. Helena Bonham Carter, Matt Damon, Jude Law, Alicia Keyes, Kanye West, Javier Bardem, Taylor Swift, Conan O'Brien and Mark Wahlberg.

Though their webpage *www.wmeentertainment.com* is useless for agency information, the voiceover link yields many voices and styles and would help create your own VO sample. WME's list of agents repping actors is below.

Agents
Mel Berger, Jim Ornstein, John Bizzetti, Jeff Googel, Jason Hodes, Henry Reisch, Sam Kirby, Erin Junkin, David Kalodner, Kirby Kim, John Rosen, Josh Bider, Ken Slotnick, Scott Wachs, Susan Weaving, Joel Zimmerman
Client List
2727 worldwide

⚞ Wolf Talent Group ⚟

165 W 46th Street, #1104
btwn 6th Avenue and Broadway
New York, NY 10036
212-840-6787

Big changes for Teresa Wolf. Formerly a partner at bicoastal Schiowitz/Connor/Ankrum/Wolf, Teresa is now the sole owner of Wolf Talent Group. An actor before Honey Sanders made her an agent, Teresa also worked at Penny Leudeke and Waters Nicolosi.

Teresa says she shares clients and is still good friends with the new west coast version of her former partners now called Connor Ankrum & Associates and Josh Schiowitz who is now a manager.

Joining Teresa is Michael Hennessy who began his agenting career with Teresa. Their assistant is Lain Kunin.

Clients from their list include Colman Domingo (*The Scottsboro Boys, A Boy & His Soul, Passing Strange, Lincoln, The Butler, Chicago, Blood Knot, Miracle at St. Anna, Red Hook Summer*), Robin de Jesus (*In the Heights, La Cage Aux Folles, Hairbrained, Elliot Loves, Gun Hill Road*), Bobby Steggert (*Ragtime, Assistance, The Grand Manner, A Minister's Wife, 110 in the Shade, The Nightingale*), Marva Hicks (*Caroline or Change, Holler if You Hear Me*), Grainger Hines (*Lincoln*), Gregory Wooddell (*The Lyons*), Sheila Tapia (*Bitter Pill, CQ/CX*), Matthew Stadelmann (*Muhammad Ali's Greatest Fight*) and James Biberi (*Drive, Dead Man Down*).

Teresa still reviews all pictures and resumes. Though they have called actors from mailings, primarily their clients were referrals from other clients, casting directors or managers. They have a strict policy of not taking anyone on who's work they haven't seen.

Agents
Teresa Wolf and Michael Hennessy
Client List
40

≤ 17 ≥

Glossary

Academy Players Directory — No longer published

Actors' Equity Membership Requirements — Rules for membership for the union covering actors for work in the theater state you must have a verifiable Equity Contract in order to join, or have been a member in good standing for at least one year in SAG-AFTRA.

Initiation fee is $1100 as of 7/1/12, payable prior to election to membership. Basic dues are $118 annually. Additionally, there are working dues: 2.25% of gross weekly earnings from employment is deducted from your check just like your income tax. Check *www.actorsequity.org* for the most up to date numbers.

Actors' Equity Minimum — There are many basic contracts ranging from the low end of the Small Production Contract to the higher Production Contract covering Broadway houses, Jones Beach, tours, etc. Highest is the Business Theater Agreement, for industrial shows produced by large corporations. Check *www.actorsequity.org*.

Actor Unions — Actors' Equity Association (AEA) covers actors' employment in the theater. SAG-AFTRA (Screen Actors Guild – The American Federation of Television and Radio Artists) covers performers for film, television, radio, broadcasters, new media, stunts and recording artists.

Atmosphere — another term for background performers, a.k.a. Extras.

Audition Tape — A DVD usually no longer than six minutes, showcasing either one performance or a montage of scenes of an actor's work. Agents and casting directors prefer tapes of professional appearances (film or television), but some will look at a tape produced for audition purposes only.

Background Performers — a.k.a. Atmosphere or Extras.

Breakdown Services — Started in 1971 by Gary Marsh, the Service condenses scripts and lists parts available in films, television and theater. Expensive and available to agents and managers only.

Clear — The unions require that the agent check with a freelance actor (clearing) before submitting him on a particular project.

Equity-Waiver Productions — See Showcases.

Freelance — Term used to describe the relationship between an actor and agent or agents who submit the actor for work without an exclusive contract. New York agents frequently will work on this basis, Los Angeles agents rarely consent to this arrangement.

Going Out — Auditions or meetings with directors and/or casting directors. These are usually set up by your agent but have also been set up by very persistent and courageous actors.

Going to Network — Final process in landing a pilot/series. After the audition process has narrowed the list of choices, actors who have already signed option deals have another callback for network executives, usually at the network. Sometimes this process can include an extra callback for the heads of whatever studio is involved.

Industry Referral — If you are looking for an agent, the best possible way to access one is if someone with some credibility in the business offers to make a phone call for you. This could be a casting director, writer, producer, or the agent's mother, as long as it's someone whose opinion the agent respects. If someone says, "just use my name," forget it. They need to offer to make a phone call for you.

The Leagues — A now defunct formal collective of prestigious theater schools offering conservatory training for the actor. There is no longer a formal association, but the current "favored" schools are still referred to by this designation. As far as agents are concerned, this is the very best background an actor can have, other than having your father own a studio.

Schools in this collective are listed on page 3.

Letter of Termination — A legal document dissolving the contract between actor and agent. Send a copy of the letter to your agent via registered mail, return receipt requested, plus a copy to SAG-AFTRA and all other unions involved. Retain a copy for your files.

Open Call — Refers to auditions or meetings held by casting directors that are not restricted by agents. No individual appointments are given. Usually the call is made in an advertisement in one of the trade newspapers, by flyers, or in a news story in the popular press. As you can imagine, the number of people that show up is enormous. You will have to wait a long time. Although management's eyes tend to glaze over and see nothing after a certain number of hours, actors do sometimes get jobs this way.

Overexposed — Term used by nervous buyers (producers, casting directors, networks, etc.) indicating an actor has become too recognizable for their tastes. Frequently he just got off another show after which everyone remembers him as that character and the buyer doesn't want the public thinking of that instead of his project. A thin line exists between not being recognizable and being overexposed.

Packaging — This practice involves a talent agency approaching a buyer with a writer, a star, usually a star director and possibly a producer already attached to it. May include any number of other writers, actors, producers, etc.

Paid Auditions — There's no formal name for the practice of rounding up twenty actors and charging them for the privilege of meeting a casting director, agent, producer, etc. There are agents, casting directors and actors who feel the practice is unethical. It does give some actors who would otherwise not be seen an opportunity to meet casting directors. I feel meeting a casting director under these circumstances is questionable and that there are more productive ways to spend your money.

Per Diem — Negotiated amount of money for expenses on location or on the road per day.

Pictures — The actor's calling card. An 8x10 glossy or matte print color or black and white photograph.

Pilot — The first episode of a proposed television series. Produced so that the network can determine whether there will be additional episodes. There are many pilots made every year. Few get picked up. Fewer stay on the air for more than a single season.

Principal — Job designation indicating a part larger than an extra or an Under Five.

Ready to Book — Agent talk for an actor who has been trained and judged mature enough to handle himself well in the audition with material and with buyers. Frequently refers to an actor whose progress in acting class or theater has been monitored by the agent.

Resume — The actor's ID: lists credits, physical description, agent's name, phone contact and special skills.

Right — When someone describes an actor as being right for a part, he is speaking about the essence of an actor. We all associate a particular essence with Brad Pitt and a different essence with Jim Carrey. One would not expect Pitt and Carrey to be up for the same part. Being right also involves credits. The more important the part, the more credits are necessary to support being seen.

Scale — The lowest contract fee a union member can work for.

SAG-AFTRA (Screen Actors Guild Membership — American Federation of Television and Radio Artists) represents more than 160,000 actors, announcers, broadcasters journalists, dancers, DJs, news writers, news editors, program hosts, puppeteers, recording artists, singers, stunt performers, voiceover artists and other media professionals.

The steps to join SAG-AFTRA are presented in detail at *www.sag.org/content/steps-join*. Basically you must work in a position covered by a SAG-AFTRA or SAG or AFTRA collective bargaining agreement (three days of work if you are a background actor) or if you are a paid up member of an affiliated performers' union (ACTRA, AEA, AGMA or AGVA) for a period of one year and have worked and been paid at least once as a principal performer in that union's jurisdiction.

Proof of employment may be in the form of a signed contract, a payroll check or check stub, or a letter from the company (on company letterhead). The document must state the applicant's name, Social Security number, name of the production or commercial, the salary paid in dollar amount, and the dates worked.

The SAG-AFTRA initiation fee as of 6-1-12 is $3,000.00, payable in full by cashier's check or money order at the time of application plus first annual dues payment of $198.00.

The fees may be lower in some branch areas. Dues are based on earnings and are billed twice a year. If you are not working, you can go on Honorary Withdrawal which only relieves you of the obligation to pay your dues. You are still in the union and prohibited from accepting non-union work. For up to the minute information on joining, dues, and many other things, visit *www.sag.org*. Search for initiation fee or for recorded information on how to join SAG or call 323-549-6772.

SAG-AFTRA Minimum — As of 7-1-12, SAG scale is $842 daily, but can be less for low budget films and interactive media. Call SAG-AFTRA contracts for specific information regarding your contract. You don't have to be a member to check.

Showcases — Productions in which members of Actors' Equity are allowed by the union to work without compensation are called Showcases in New York and 99-Seat Theater Plan in Los Angeles. Equity members are allowed to perform, as long as the productions conform to certain Equity guidelines: rehearsal conditions, limiting the number of performances and seats, and providing a set number of complimentary tickets for industry people. The producers must provide tickets for franchised agents, casting directors and producers.

Sides — The pages of script containing your audition material. Usually not enough information to use as a source to do a good audition. If they won't give you a complete script, go early (or the day before), sit in the office and read it. SAG rules require producers to allow actors access to the script if it's written.

Stage Time — Term used to designate the amount of time a performer has had in front of an audience. Most agents and casting executives believe that an actor can only achieve a certain level of confidence by amassing stage time. They're right.

Submissions — Sending an actor's name to a casting director in hopes of getting the actor an audition or meeting for a part.

Talent — Management's synonym for actors.

Test Option Agreement — Before going to network for a final call back for a pilot/series, actors must routinely sign a contract that negotiates salary for the pilot and for the series. The contract is usually for five years with a option for two more years. All options are at the discretion of management. They can drop you at the end of any season. You are bound by the terms of your contract to stay for the initial five years plus their two one-year options.

Top of the Show/Major Role — A predetermined fee set by producers which is a non-negotiable maximum for guest appearances on television episodes. Also called Major Role Designation.

The Trades — *Backstage* and *Call Sheet* are newspapers that cover all kinds of show business. See page 38 for more detail.

Under Five — A SAG-AFTRA job in which the actor has five or fewer lines. Paid at a specific rate less than a principal and more than an extra. Sometimes referred to as Five and Under.

Visible/Visibility — Currently on view in film, theater or television. In this business, it's out of sight, out of mind, so visibility is very important.

99-Seat Theater Plan — The Los Angeles version of the Showcase. Originally called waiver. Producers give actors an expense reimbursement of $5-$14 per performance. It's not much, but it adds up; at least you're not working for free.

Producers must also conform to Equity guidelines regarding rehearsal conditions, number of performances, complimentary tickets for industry, etc. If you participate in this plan, be sure to stop by Equity and get a copy of your rights.

✄ 17 ✄

Indexes

⚖ Index to Agents & Agencies ⚖

About Artists Agency. 139
About Face. 140
Abrahams, Jed. 17, 18, 45, 92, 197
Abrams Artists Agency. 141
Adelman, Phil. 33, 92, 94, 128, 129, 165
Adelman, Wendie Relkin. 165
Altman, Neal. 141
Altman, Rachel. 141
Anderson, Beverly. 76
Andreadis Talent Agency, Inc.. 143
Andreadis, Barbara. 143
Ann Steele Agency. 145
Ann Wright Representatives. 144
Archer King, Ltd. 146
Artists Group. 147
Atlas Talent. 148
Attermann, Robert. 141
Bankoff, Lisa. 173
Bauman, Redanty & Shaul. 149
Beckner, Kyetay. 166
Bell, Joanna. 170
Berger, Mel. 201
Berkowitz, Mark. 142
Bernstein, Bonnie. 173
Bider, Josh. 201
Birge, Don. 8, 196
Bizzetti, John. 201
Blickers, Beth.. 141
bloc. 150
Bodner, Charles. 149
Boone, Michael Kelly. 182
Bresler, Sandy. 86
Bret Adams. 151
Brewer, Jenevieve. 140
Brown, Megan. 142
Busch, Dianne. 91, 99, 182
Busch, Justin. 190

Butler, Alex. 172
CAA/Creative Artists Agency. 152
Carlton, Goddard and Freer Talent, Inc. 156
Carry Company. 153
Carry, Sharon. 14, 153
Carson, Nancy. 154
Carson-Adler Agency, Inc. 154
Carson/Kolker Organization. 155
Cash, David. 185
Castellanos, Erin. 187
Clear Talent Group. 157
Coleman, Ben. 189
Condon, Mackenzie. 152
Copeland, Ian. 164
Cornerstone Talent. 158
Crombie, David. 198
Curtin, Nancy. 170
Curtis, Nancy. 99, 106
Daly, Jim. 150
Davidson, Brian. 175
DDO Artists Agency. 159
Del Duca, Francis. 163
Delawder, Danielle. 141
Deroski, Bonnie. 154
DGRW/Douglas, Gorman, Rothacker & Wilhelm, Inc. 160
Dicce, Ginger. 167
DiMauro, Maury. 175
Don Buchwald & Associates 161
Dornbaum, Jeffrey. 177
Dorothy Palmer Talent Agency, Inc. 162
Douglas, Sarah. 141
Doussant, Diana. 17, 45, 46, 92, 99, 182
Edwards, Scott. 170
Epstein, Gary. 103, 190
Esposito, Genine. 141
Faison, Shirley. 154
Fargo, Sarah. 187
Fifi Oscard Agency, Inc. 163
Finn, Heather. 164

Fisher, Steven. 173
Flores, Dustin. 198
Flynn, Jim. 28, 48, 91, 92, 176
Fox, Jason. 152
Frontier Booking International, Inc. 164
Gage Group.. 165
Gage, Martin. 61, 90, 98, 126, 165
Gersh Agency New York. 166
Gersh, Gary.. 175
Gilbert, Ellen.. 141
Gill, Jeffrey. 177
Ginger Dicce Talent Agency. 167
Glicker, Renee.. . . . . 17, 91, 93, 139
Goldberg, Ellie. 100, 101, 126, 180
Goldblum, Tracey.. 141
Goldman, Pam. 161
Goldstein, Randi.. 166
Googel, Jeff.. 201
Gotham Talent Agency.. 168
Green, Simon. 152
Griffin, Jim. 187
Guy, Michael.. 148
Gwiazda, Ron. 141
Hadley, Peggy. 188
Hanns Wolters International. 169
Harden, Mary. 170
Harden-Curtis Associates. 170
Harris, Jamie. 157
Hashagan, Fred.. 187
Henderson-Hogan Agency.. 172
Hennessy, Michael. 202
Hess, Peter.. 152
Highland, Christopher. 187
Hilepo, Paul.. 171
Hirsh, Stephen.. 166
Hodes, Jason. 201
Hossenlopp, John. 148
Hunter, Jeff.. . . . . 48, 50, 91, 93, 127
ICM Partners.. 173
Ingber & Associates. 174

Ingber, Carole. 174
Ingegno, Tom. 111
Innovative Artists. 175
Isler, Zach. 173
Jebens, B. Lynne. 181
Jenness, Morgan. 141
Jim Flynn, Inc. 176
Jordon Gill & Dornbaum Agency, Inc.. 177
Judy Boals, Inc.. 178
Junkin, Erin. 201
Kahn, Jerry. 55
Kaiser, Pete. 197
Kalodner, David. 201
Kane, Jay. 43, 92, 99, 100, 200
Kaplan, Kenneth. 55, 61, 86, 103
Kastrup, Kevin. 187
Katz, Cynthia.. 168
Kelly, Shannon. 158
Kerin - Goldberg Associates. 180
Kerin, Charles. 100, 180
Kim, Kirby.. 201
King, Archer. 46, 146
Kirby, Sam.. 201
Kirsten, Michael. 170
Kolker, Barry.. 155
Konawall, Jennifer.. 166
Krasner, David. 198
Krasny Office, Inc.. 181
Krasny, Gary. 14, 48, 65, 79, 100, 101, 104, 121, 124, 126, 181
Kress, Victoria.. 161
La Via, Carmen. 163
Lally, Dale. 184
Larner, Lionel. 48
Laviska, Stephen. 184
Leading Artists, Inc.. 182
Lee, Ken. 175
Leiner, Jeremy. 185
Lesser, Ian. 148
Leudeke Agency. 183

Levy, Allison. 175
Lewis, Cara. 152
Lewis, David. 161
Lichtman, Juliana.. 157
Lieberman, Lisa. 175
Lockhorn, Jeffrey. 189
LTA/Lally Talent Agency. 184
Lubliner, Sheldon. 192
Luedeke, Penny. 183
Lutsch, George. 172
Machota, Joe. 152
Mahrdt, Oliver.. 169
Maihack, Steve.. 196
Malcolm, Robert. 147
Manners, Scott.. 195
Manning, Brian. 152
Marber-Rich, Lisa. 148
Marshall, Timothy. 149
Martino, Paul.. 173
Mason, Jonathan. 161
Mazur, Amy. 141
McDermott, David. 177
McGunigle, Diane.. 152
McKeon, Meredith. 148
McPherson, Barry. 142
McShane, Kevin. 163
Melamed, Ken.. 151
Menasche, Jack. 46
Micone, Ed. 187
Milam, Thompson.. 172
Mills, Johathan.. 187
Misher, Jaime.. 175
Mishico, Maegan. 150
Navin, Kate. 141
Nichols, Chris. 181
Nici, Joanne.. 161
Nicolosi & Co. Inc.. 185
Nicolosi, Jeanne. 16, 99, 185
O'Brien, Tim.. 157
Olshan, Ricki.. 161

Ornstein, Jim. 201
Oscard, Fifi. 71, 163
Ostler, Bruce. 151
Paciullo, Stephanie. 152
Palmer, Dorothy. 162
Pamplin, H. Shep. 48, 61
Pantera, Meg. 186
Paradigm. 187
Pearl, Josh. 173
Peggy Hadley Enterprises. 188
Peter Strain & Associates 189
Phoenix Artists. 190
Pisetsky, Chad. 160
Poeta, Paula. 157
Price, Lisa. 17, 191
Price, Rhonda. 166
Professional Artists. 192
Pultz, Josh. 160
Quinoa, Dannielle. 175
Raider, Honey. 199
Redanty, Mark. 149
Reisch, Henry. 201
Reisman, Paul. 141
Riley, Diane. 170
Rodriquez, Michael. 193
Rosen, John. 201
Rosier, Liz. 171
Ross, Randy. 190
Ross, Ron. 180
Roundtree, Margi. 151
Rudes, Jerry. 163
Sage, Tim. 187
Sands, Ben. 195
Schlegel, Mark. 158
Schmenner, Richard. 187
Schweitzer, Adam. 173
Scott, Marilynn. 192
Scott, Thomas. 17, 39, 159
Serow, Billy. 141

Shea, John. 164
Sheedy, Rachel. 161
Sheplin - Winik Artists. 194
Shumofsky, Bonnie. 141
Skiba, Alice. 140
Slotnick, Ken. 201
Smith, Bruce. 110, 111
Smith, Matthew. 187
Starkman, Marvin. 76
Steele, Ann. 45, 145
Stevens, Clifford. 187
Stewart Talent. 196
Stewart, Jane. 196
Stewart, Sonia. 140
Stone Manners Salners. 195
Stone, Steve. 158
Stone, Tim. 195
Strain, Peter. 108
Suchoff, Noah. 148
Sutfin, Phil. 173
Talent House, The. 197
Talent Representatives, Inc. 199
Talentworks New York. 200
Tantleff, Jack. 201
Tanzer, Scott. 196
Teitelbaum, Maura. 141
Tellez, Steve. 111
The Price Group Talent. 191
Thompson, Joe. 141
Timms, Bill. 45, 48, 90, 99, 189
Turner, Mark. 141
Unger, Steve. 165
Veloric, Bill. 175
Vizcaino, Huascar. 155
Volkman, Kara. 196
Wachs, Scott. 201
Wagner, Amy. 141
Wasser, John. 148
Watenberg, Eric. 152
Watson, Emily. 150

Weaving, Susan. 201
Weiss, Tracy. 141
Wichinsky, Nicole. 160
Wilhelm, Jim. 25, 93, 100, 160
Williams, Ashley. 192
Willig, Alan. 161
Wilson, Fatima. 150
WME/William Morris Endeavor 201
Wolf Talent Group. 202
Wolf, Teresa. 202
Wolters, Hanns. 169
Wright, Ann. 144
Wright, Susan. 144
Yoselow, Scott. 166
Zedek, David. 152
Zimmerman, Joel. 201

◢ Index to Agents for Children ◣

Abrams Artists Agency. 141
Andreadis Talent Agency, Inc. 143
Carson-Adler Agency, Inc. 154
Carson/Kolker Organization. 155
Don Buchwald & Associates 161
Frontier Booking International, Inc. 164
ICM Partners. 173
Jordon Gill & Dornbaum Agency, Inc. 177
WME/William Morris Endeavor 201
Wright, Ann. 144

◢ Index to Agents for Standups ◣

About Artists Agency. 139
APA/Agency for the Performing Arts. 142
CAA 152
Cornerstone Talent. 158
ICM Partners. 173
Innovative Artists. 175
WME/William Morris Endeavor 201

⋈ Index to Agents for Young Adults ⋈

Abrams Artists Agency.................................... 141
Andreadis Talent Agency, Inc............................. 143
APA/Agency for the Performing Arts. 142
Carson-Adler Agency, Inc................................. 154
Carson/Kolker Organization.............................. 155
Don Buchwald & Associates. 161
Frontier Booking International, Inc. 164
ICM Partners... 173
Jordon Gill & Dornbaum Agency, Inc..................... 177
Sheplin - Winik Artists. 194
WME/William Morris Endeavor 201
Wright, Ann.. 144

⋈ Index to Agents for Dancers ⋈

bloc. 150
DDO Artists Agency. 159
Leudeke Agency. 183
Scott, Thomas.. 17, 39

⋈ Index to Dance Teachers ⋈

Bam Bam... 33
Broadway Dance Center................................... 33
Drew. 33
Feliciano, Angel.. 33
HB Studios. 32
Jones, George. 33
Peters, Kelly... 33
Rhapsody... 33
Ripley Grier Studios. 33
Soraya... 33
Steps.. 33

✍ Index to Everything Else ✍

90%-10%. 98
99-Seat Theater Plan. 208
Academy Players Directory. 203
Access and Stature. 95
Actor-friendly neighborhoods. 12
Actors' Equity Membership Requirements. 203
Actors' Equity Minimum. 203
Actors' Unions. 203
Agent Meetings. 72
Agent Research. 69-71
Agent Stereotypes. 133
Agents' Expectations. 103
Atmosphere. 203
Audition Tape. 203
Background Performers. 204
Breakdown Service. 204
Casting Society of America Job File. 14
Cool Schools. 3
Definitive Client. 90
Drama Book Shop. 12
Equity Membership Requirements. 203
Equity Open Calls. 25
Equity-Waiver Productions. 204
Exclusive Representation. 65
Financial Core. 34
Freelance. 204
Going Out. 204
Going to Network. 204
Guide to Cross Streets. 12
Important Details. 101
Jobs. 13
Kevin Bacon/Referrals. 136
Leagues. 204
Letter of Termination. 205
MetroCards. 11
National Conference of Personal Managers. 120

Number of Clients. 134
Open Calls. 25, 205
Overexposed. 205
Packaging. 205
Paid Auditions. 205
Paragraph 6. 66
Per Diem. 205
Photographers. 21
Pictures. 19, 205
Pilot. 206
Principal. 206
Process. 54
Reading List. 40
Ready to Book. 206
Reality 51
Reel Power. 41, 87
Reference Library. 40
Resume. 22, 24, 206
Right. 206
Scale. 206
Set-Sitters. 114
Showcases. 33, 207
Sides. 207
Size. 94
Stage Time. 207
Submissions. 208
Support Groups. 30
Talent. 46, 208
Teachers. 31
Test Option Agreement. 208
Theatrical vs. Commercial Representation. 65
Top of the Show/Major Role. 208
Trades. 208
Under Five. 208
Unions. 34
Visible/Visibility. 208
Working as an Extra. 37

◢ Index to Mentors ◣

Anderson, Beverly.......................... 52, 54, 56, 76, 90, 128
Angle, Tim................................... 29, 52, 53, 55, 104
Beddingfield, Ric.. 106
Douglas, Barry... 51
Duchovny, David... 56
Field, Sally... 52
Kingman, Michael.. 91
Litwak, Mark.. 79, 87
Oliver, Lynn Moore.. 62
Oscard, Fifi... 52, 71, 129
Parseghian, Gene... 80, 86, 94
Ross, Joanna.. 8, 59
Starkman, Marvin... 50, 76, 93, 94
Walton, Laurie... 92, 100, 107
Weaver, Sigourney... 49, 54
Wolfe, George... 49
Woods, James... 85, 87

◢ Index to Photographers ◣

Blinkoff, Richard... 21
Coleman, Nick... 20, 21
Cross, Dave.. 21
Dauk, Jinsey... 22
Steinkolk, Tess.. 21

◢ Index to Resources ◣

Actors Access... 38, 39
Affordable Housing... 12
Backstage.. 38
Breakdown Services............................... 39, 42, 62, 204
Call Sheet... 38
Dancers' Alliance.. 42
Ibdb.com.. 40, 70

Imdbpro.com. 134
New York Counseling Center. 38
Ross Reports Television & Film. 38
SAG-AFTRA Information for Kids. 114
SAG-AFTRA Initiation Fee. 206
SAG-AFTRA Membership Requirements. 206
Showbusiness Weekly. 39
Showfax. 38
Visitor's Bureau. 12

◢ Index to Teachers ◣

Beckson, JoAnna. 31
Esper, William. 31
HB Studio. 32
Ludwig, Karen. 32
Miller, Allan. 32
Terry Shreiber Studios 32

☑ Endnotes ☒

1. "Top 25 Drama Schools", May 11, 2012

2. "Acting Is One Thing, Getting Hired Another," May 25, 1997

3. "Acting Is One Thing, Getting Hired Another," May 25, 1997

4. "The Early Bird Gets the Audition," March 23, 1995

5. "The Early Bird Gets the Audition," March 23, 1995

6. "The Careerist's Guide to Survival," April 25, 1982

7. "Out from the Shadows," January 13, 2000

8. "Out from the Shadows," January 13, 2000

9. "The Careerist Guide to Survival," April 25, 1982

10. "Out from the Shadows," January 13, 2000

11. "Hiding in Plain Sight," May 1997

12. "Out of the Woods", November 1994

13. Ibid.

14. Silman-James Press, 2002

15. "Young, Famous and Vulnerable", November 6, 2010

16. Ibid.

17. "Do Re Me Me Me!," November 10, 1997

18. " What You Really Need to Know about Managers and Talent Agents,"
    A Practical Guide, March, 2001

19. "J. Lo: Ex-manager violated," July 3, 2003

20. "Vardalos' Ex--manager Dealt Lawsuit Setback," September 17, 2003